FOUNDATION AND AUTHORITY

A LAYMAN'S INTRODUCTION TO THE
WESTMINSTER CONFESSION OF FAITH

FOUNDATION AND AUTHORITY

holding life and reality together

CHARLES H. DUNAHOO

METOKOS PRESS

Metokos Press
211 Main Street, suite 108
Narrows, VA 24124

Published by Metokos Press, Inc., committed to providing materials easily
accessible to the average reader while at the same time presenting biblical truth
from within the framework of biblical and confessional churches of the
reformed and Presbyterian heritage. Visit u s on the web at:

www.metokospress.com

Cover design by John Dunahoo, Atlanta, GA
Interior deign and layout by Scribe Freelance, Bronx, NY

Printed in the United States by Lightning Source, LaVergne, TN

ISBN 978-0-9786955-1-4

Preface

THERE WERE TWO PERIODS in church history when the church made its mark and established firm foundations to the Christian faith. The first period was in the early church when the church councils formulated and articulated some of the basic and essential doctrines taught in scripture. For example: the clear teaching on the two natures of Christ, or the Trinity, or the relation of Christ the Son to God the father. Those foundational truths have sustained the church for centuries.

The second period of the 15th and 16th centuries marks the Protestant Reformation times. Confessions and creeds were developed that set forth the essentials of biblical Christianity—the Heidelberg Catechism, the Belgic Confession, the Canons of Dordt, and the Westminster Standards were among some of those confessional documents that were expressions of the church's commitment to Scripture and its authority. Each of the church councils and each of the confessions and creeds have brought their uniqueness to Christianity and the church; however, the Westminster Confession and Faith and Catechisms were unique not because they taught something different from the others, but of all the early council's formulations of doctrine and later the Protestant and Reformed Confessions and Catechisms, the Westminster Confession of Faith began with a clear statement on the Scriptures. While those named above certainly reflected biblical truth, the Westminster Divines chose to begin with Scripture, even prior to its doctrinal confession about God.

While some have argued that Westminster should have started with the doctrine of God, the writers chose to begin with the infallible and inspired Word of God where we learn about God is a special and covenantal way. Without beginning with Scripture, you always run the risk of talking about the wrong god. Though God reveals himself in a general way through his creation to all of his creatures, through his Word, he especially reveals himself to us in a way that enables us to know him as he wants to be known. The Psalmist reminds us that it is not what we think about God that matters so much but rather what God tells us about himself. To paraphrase David's words in Psalm 139: 17, "it is not my thoughts about God but God's thoughts about himself that really matters."

A second thing the WCF addresses in the opening chapter is a topic that is particularly timely today and that is who interprets Scripture? Does the author or the reader determine the meaning of Scripture? The WCF makes clear that finally and ultimately the only infallible interpreter of Scripture is Scripture itself. The meaning is determined by God, the author of the text and not the reader or human interpreter, though they are part of the process. This means that the Scriptures cannot mean what we want them to mean but only what God intended to reveal to us. The words of Scripture were inspired by God therefore what Scripture says in nothing less than the word of God.

A third thing the WCF does in this opening and foundational chapter is to assure us that the words of Scripture are not simply words that men wrote which God at sometime or other may or may not choose to make alive to the reader or hearer. Though they are words penned by the human authors, they are the very word of God, not written in some mechanical dictation method but supernaturally written as God breathed out his words through men. While it is true that when we are talking about the supernatural and there are things that we will never fully comprehend, the Scriptures are given, along with the Holy Spirit, to teach us, to correct us when wrong, to instruct us in righteous living.

As we read through the WCF and its accompanying documents, one has to marvel how God used the Westminster Divines to carefully, meticulously, and thoroughly give us the system of doctrine that has become the hallmark of biblical doctrine among Christians for over 400 years.

Chapter One
OF THE HOLY SCRIPTURE

CONFESSION OF FAITH

1. Although the light of nature, and the works of creation and providence do so far manifest the goodness, wisdom, and power of God, as to leave men unexcusable; yet are they not sufficient to give that knowledge of God, and of his will, which is necessary unto salvation. Therefore it pleased the Lord, at sundry times, and in divers manners, to reveal himself, and to declare that his will unto his church; and afterwards, for the better preserving and propagating of the truth, and for the more sure establishment and comfort of the church against the corruption of the flesh, and the malice of Satan and of the world, to commit the same wholly unto writing: which maketh the Holy Scripture to be most necessary; those former ways of God's revealing his will unto his people being now ceased.

2. Under the name of Holy Scripture, or the Word of God written, are now contained all the books of the Old and New Testaments, which are these:

Of the Old Testament:

Genesis	II Chronicles	Daniel
Exodus	Ezra	Hosea
Leviticus	Nehemiah	Joel
Numbers	Esther	Amos
Deuteronomy	Job	Obadiah
Joshua	Psalms	Jonah
Judges	Proverbs	Micah
Ruth	Ecclesiastes	Nahum
I Samuel	The Song of Songs	Habakkuk
II Samuel	Isaiah	Zephaniah
I Kings	Jeremiah	Haggai
II Kings	Lamentations	Zechariah
I Chronicles	Ezekiel	Malachi

Of the New Testament:

The Gospels According to:	Galatians	*The Epistle of:*
	Ephesians	James
Matthew	Philippians	*The First and Second Epistles of:*
Mark	Colossians	
Luke	Thessalonians I	Peter
John	Thessalonians II	*The First, Second, and Third Epistles of:*
The Acts of the Apostles	*to* Timothy I	
Paul's Epistles to the:	*to* Timothy II	John
	to Titus	*The Epistle of:*
Romans	*to* Philemon	Jude
Corinthians I	*The Epistle to the:*	*The Revelation of John*
Corinthians II	Hebrews	

All which are given by inspiration of God to be the rule of faith and life.

3. The books commonly called Apocrypha, not being of divine inspiration, are no part of the canon of the Scripture, and therefore are of no authority in the church of God, nor to be any otherwise approved, or made use of, than other human writings.

4. The authority of the Holy Scripture, for which it ought to be believed, and obeyed, dependeth not upon the testimony of any man, or church; but wholly upon God (who is truth itself) the author thereof: and therefore it is to be received, because it is the Word of God.

5. We may be moved and induced by the testimony of the church to an high and reverent esteem of the Holy Scripture. And the heavenliness of the matter, the efficacy of the doctrine, the majesty of the style, the consent of all the parts, the scope of the whole (which is, to give all glory to God), the full discovery it makes of the only way of man's salvation, the many other incomparable excellencies, and the entire perfection thereof, are arguments whereby it doth abundantly evidence itself to be the Word of God: yet notwithstanding, our full persuasion and assurance of the infallible truth and divine authority thereof, is from the inward work of the Holy Spirit bearing witness by and with the Word in our hearts.

6. The whole counsel of God concerning all things necessary for his own glory, man's salvation, faith and life, is either expressly set down in Scripture, or by good and necessary consequence may be deduced from Scripture: unto which nothing at any time is to be added, whether by new revelations of the Spirit, or traditions of men. Nevertheless, we acknowledge the inward illumination of the Spirit of God to be necessary for the saving understanding of such things as are revealed in the Word: and that there are some circumstances concerning the worship of God, and government of the church, common to human actions and societies, which are to be ordered by the light of nature, and Christian prudence, according to the general rules of the Word, which are always to be observed.

7. All things in Scripture are not alike plain in themselves, nor alike clear unto all: yet those things which are necessary to be known, believed, and observed for salvation, are so clearly propounded, and opened in some place of Scripture or other, that not only the learned, but the unlearned, in a due use of the ordinary means, may attain unto a sufficient understanding of them.

8. The Old Testament in Hebrew (which was the native language of the people of God of old), and the New Testament in Greek (which, at the time of the writing of it, was most generally known to the nations), being immediately inspired by God, and, by his singular care and providence, kept pure in all ages, are therefore authentical; so as, in all controversies of religion, the church is finally to appeal unto them. But, because these original tongues are not known to all the people of God, who have right unto, and interest in the Scriptures, and are commanded, in the fear of God, to read and search them, therefore they are to be translated into the vulgar language of every nation unto which they come, that, the Word of God dwelling plentifully in all, they may worship him in an acceptable manner; and, through patience and comfort of the Scriptures, may have hope.

9. The infallible rule of interpretation of Scripture is the Scripture itself: and therefore, when there is a question about the true and full sense of any Scripture (which is not manifold, but one), it must be searched and known by other places that speak more clearly.

10. The supreme judge by which all controversies of religion are to be determined, and all decrees of councils, opinions of ancient writers, doctrines of men, and private spirits, are to be examined, and in whose sentence we are to rest, can be no other but the Holy Spirit speaking in the Scripture.

THE WESTMINSTER DIVINES, in the opening chapter of the Westminster Confession, firmly establish the priority of the Scriptures of the Old and New Testaments in all of the doctrines taught in the chapters that follow. In so doing, the divines emphasize the need we have for the Scriptures to be preserved and utilized just as God has given them.

They recognize the point the apostle Paul made in the opening chapter of Romans: that though the truth about God is clearly proclaimed in all that God has made and does, yet, because of sin, men are unable to benefit from this truth by coming to God in faith. Men and women need something more than God's revelation in the world around us, and God has provided his written Word as our guide for life and faith. While the Westminster Confession of Faith represents the foundation and authority of the Christian faith, the Bible is the foundation and authority for the confession.

The divines affirm the sixty-six books of Scripture as God's infallible Word written, the only place where the way to God and the way to salvation are taught infallibly. They go on to say that we are assured of this by the testimony of the Holy Spirit bearing witness by the Word in our hearts, and not merely by councils or pronouncements of fallible men or churches.

We are assured, as was the author of the Nineteenth Psalm, that the Scriptures are complete (perfect), lacking nothing necessary for God's glory or for our salvation, faith, and life. Though it contains many things difficult to understand, everything necessary for salvation is so clearly taught that even the uneducated can understand and come to God through faith, by the teachings of Scripture.

The divines further assure us that Scripture has been preserved through the ages free from human defects, in the original languages

(Hebrew and Greek), and is available to all in the modern tongues of mankind.

They say that the infallible interpretation of any passage of Scripture is found in Scripture itself and not in the opinions of men, so the final authority in all controversies of men and religions is *only* the Holy Spirit who has spoken in Scripture.

Chapter Two

OF GOD AND THE HOLY TRINITY

CONFESSION OF FAITH

1. There is but one only, living, and true God, who is infinite in being and perfection, a most pure spirit, invisible, without body, parts, or passions; immutable, immense, eternal, incomprehensible, almighty, most wise, most holy, most free, most absolute; working all things according to the counsel of his own immutable and most righteous will, for his own glory; most loving, gracious, merciful, long-suffering, abundant in goodness and truth, forgiving iniquity, transgression, and sin; the rewarder of them that diligently seek him; and withal, most just, and terrible in his judgments, hating all sin, and who will by no means clear the guilty.

2. God hath all life, glory, goodness, blessedness, in and of himself; and is alone in and unto himself all-sufficient, not standing in need of any creatures which he hath made, nor deriving any glory from them, but only manifesting his own glory in, by, unto, and upon them. He is the alone fountain of all being, of whom, through whom, and to whom are all things; and hath most sovereign dominion over them, to do by them, for them, or upon them whatsoever himself pleaseth. In his sight all things are open and manifest, his knowledge is infinite, infallible, and independent upon the creature, so as nothing is to him contingent, or uncertain. He is most holy in all his counsels, in all his works, and in all his commands. To him is due from angels and men, and every other creature, whatsoever worship, service, or obedience he is pleased to require of them.

3. In the unity of the Godhead there be three persons, of one substance, power, and eternity: God the Father, God the Son, and God the Holy Ghost: the Father is of none, neither begotten, nor proceeding; the Son is eternally begotten of the Father; the Holy Ghost eternally proceeding from the Father and the Son.

THE WESTMINSTER CONFESSION of Faith is a beautiful summary of the doctrines contained in the Word of God. Its brevity in making an inclusive statement of the biblical faith makes it a most valuable confession. Thus after dealing with the doctrine of Scripture, the divines move next to the doctrine of God.

The second chapter of the confession is a good example of how much the divines are able to say in precise language. There can be found no clearer summary of the doctrine of God, his attributes, and his counsel.

This summary is simple in form, deep in content, and faithful in subject matter. The first paragraph deals with the biblical definition of God, his person, attributes, and will. This is the living and true God who is absolute perfection. The superlatives in the first paragraph distinguish him from any false god or false idea of God.

The doctrine of God is foundational. It underlies every other teaching. Much more could have been said about him in paragraphs one and two, but nothing can surpass these statements for a summary of the doctrine of God. The way they are developed makes it clear that the God of Scripture is unique. He is not a creature of time and chance. He does not change with every blowing wind. He is absolutely dependable.

One could take the descriptive words in the first two paragraphs and develop an interesting Bible study. Such a study would be valuable for people plagued with "the God problem"—the problem of just who or what is God—both inside and outside the church.

It is hard for some believers to realize that many people do not even have a biblical picture of God, but think of him either in human terms, or else as so removed from his creation that he is effectively silent.

A student who understands paragraphs one and two will have a healthy perspective about God. God's incommunicable attributes, i.e., those characteristics that man cannot have because they are unique to God, remind us that he is the high and lofty One, unlike every creature. These incommunicable attributes include his immutability (God does not change), infinitude (he is present everywhere at the same time), independence (he does not depend on anybody or anything), and incomprehensibility (we cannot fully understand God), among others. He is the Creator and thus not part of his creation. God's communicable attributes, on the other hand, are those characteristics of God that man can have. These communicable attributes include his being, wisdom, power, holiness, truth, and so forth. God can and does communicate (pass along) these attributes to men and women.

God's incommunicable attributes stress his uniqueness and transcenddence in relation with all of creation. He is unlike us in these ways. His communicable attributes underscore his likeness to creation and those aspects of his nature that man can experience and share.

Without an understanding of both God's standing above and outside creation as well as his presence in creation, you do not have a true concept of the living and true God of the Bible.

The third paragraph, which deals with the Trinity, summarizes what Scripture says about the differences among the three persons of the Godhead. Our God is a tri-unity, one God existing in three persons.

As the doctrine of God is essential to true faith, so is the doctrine of the Trinity fundamental to an acceptable belief in God. This section talks about the ontological aspect of the Trinity, i.e., the Trinity as it exists in reality. The Father, the Son, and the Holy Spirit are of one substance, power, and glory. There is no subordination of persons in the Godhead. They have different responsibilities in creation and redemption, but in their essence they are equal.

This doctrine of the Tri-unity of God is the focal point of the Christian faith; so one would naturally expect that every heresy has stemmed from some perversion of this doctrine. When someone suggests that the Son and the Holy Spirit are less in supremacy than God the Father, he has a deficient view of the Son and the Holy Spirit.

We believe in God the Father, God the Son, and God the Holy Spirit. We cannot emphasize the Fatherhood of God only, as do the Unitarians; nor can we simply talk about Jesus or christocentric (Christ-centered) theology, as do the neoorthodox; nor can we merely dwell on the Holy Spirit as do the Pentecostals. Ours is a Triune God, and the persons of the Godhead are the same in substance and equal in power and glory.

Chapter Two, paragraphs one and two, teach that there is but one living and true God, and describes him clearly. Paragraph three teaches that God is a Triune being. It teaches not only that the Father is God, but also that the Son and the Holy Spirit are equally God. These three are distinct persons but equal in substance, power, and glory.

The doctrine of the Tri-unity of God is taught in both the Old and New Testaments. The Bible is our proof of the nature of God. We have no other infallible source that draws together such an amount of material with such consistency.

Human logic must always bow to God's revelation. This chapter reminds us that God is both incomprehensible and knowable, that we can never—not even in heaven—know everything about God, but that we can know him personally and truly.

A good study of this chapter would be profitable for churches and individuals alike. It would be a strong deterrent to those who would reduce God to microscopic proportions.

Chapter Three
OF GOD'S ETERNAL DECREE

CONFESSION OF FAITH

1. God, from all eternity, did, by the most wise and holy counsel of his own will, freely, and unchangeably ordain whatsoever comes to pass: yet so, as thereby neither is God the author of sin, nor is violence offered to the will of the creatures; nor is the liberty or contingency of second causes taken away, but rather established.

2. Although God knows whatsoever may or can come to pass upon all supposed conditions, yet hath he not decreed anything because he foresaw it as future, or as that which would come to pass upon such conditions.

3. By the decree of God, for the manifestation of his glory, some men and angels are predestinated unto everlasting life; and others foreordained to everlasting death.

4. These angels and men, thus predestinated, and foreordained, are particularly and unchangeably designed, and their number so certain and definite, that it cannot be either increased or diminished.

5. Those of mankind that are predestinated unto life, God, before the foundation of the world was laid, according to his eternal and immutable purpose, and the secret counsel and good pleasure of his will, hath chosen, in Christ, unto everlasting glory, out of his mere free grace and love, without any foresight of faith, or good works, or perseverance in either of them, or any other thing in the creature, as conditions, or causes moving him thereunto; and all to the praise of his glorious grace.

6. As God hath appointed the elect unto glory, so hath he, by the eternal and most free purpose of his will, foreordained all the means thereunto. Wherefore, they who are elected, being fallen in Adam, are redeemed by Christ, are effectually called unto faith in Christ by his Spirit working in due season, are justified, adopted, sanctified, and kept by his power, through faith, unto

salvation. Neither are any other redeemed by Christ, effectually called, justified, adopted, sanctified, and saved, but the elect only.

7.   The rest of mankind God was pleased, according to the unsearchable counsel of his own will, whereby he extendeth or withholdeth mercy, as he pleaseth, for the glory of his sovereign power over his creatures, to pass by; and to ordain them to dishonor and wrath for their sin, to the praise of his glorious justice.

8.   The doctrine of this high mystery of predestination is to be handled with special prudence and care, that men, attending the will of God revealed in his Word, and yielding obedience thereunto, may, from the certainty of their effectual vocation, be assured of their eternal election. So shall this doctrine afford matter of praise, reverence, and admiration of God; and of humility, diligence, and abundant consolation to all that sincerely obey the gospel.

EACH CHAPTER IN THE WESTMINSTER Confession of Faith is masterful in the manner in which it summarizes, decently and in order, a particular doctrine of Scripture. It has been said that most of the disagreements with the confession's statements are more with the scriptural passages from which the summaries are drawn. Such may be the case all too often. However, we assume that difficulties with the doctrines come more from not having been taught them, rather than from any earlier rejection by someone with an unteachable spirit. In working to overcome such rejection of doctrine and Scripture, the Presbyterian Church in America and other Reformed churches build up the faith of believers and teach the truths of God's Word while applying the principles of the confession to the lives of people.

No doctrine was revealed either to offend or to hurt one of God's own, yet there are times—such as our conversion to the faith and our discovery of the joy of a personal walk with God—that we are so zealous for others to know the Lord and His Word that we press forward too hard and we offend some people. This is not caused by the Lord or his doctrine, but by the manner and method of the servant. Such distinction should be kept in mind.

The third chapter of the confession is about one of those subjects that have caused no small amount of trouble to some people. You could well expect it, because the truths are so precious and assuring. Our adversary seeks to erect stumbling block after stumbling block to hinder our seeing, believing, and understanding.

The wise men of the Westminster Assembly plotted their course well. They followed the written Word of God. This is why Chapter One deals with the subject of Scripture. If God's Word is not our plumb line and final authority, then we have no point of agreement or predicate of knowledge.

The Westminster divines moved faithfully and orderly to set forth the biblical faith in a reasonable manner to assist believers in knowing the Word. If we could have made one suggestion in the third chapter, it would have been to place the concluding paragraph at the beginning. "The doctrine of this high mystery of predestination is to be handled with special prudence and care, that men, attending the will of God revealed in His word, and yielding obedience thereunto, may, from the certainty of their effectual vocation, be assured of their eternal election. So shall this doctrine afford matter of praise, reverence, and admiration of God, and of humility, diligence, and abundant consolation, to all that sincerely obey the Gospel."

In studying the decrees of God, it is helpful to see the sequence of development in Chapter Three. The chapter teaches the truth that God is in complete control of all things that happen, but that man is always responsible before God for his words, thoughts, and deeds.

The first two paragraphs deal with God's sovereign decrees and their all-inclusiveness regarding creation. In creation, nothing happens outside the sovereign will of God. Nor does God will something to happen simply because he foresees it as happening in the future through some cause other than himself. Things happen because of God's will. He is the moving force in all of creation, but in a way that does not remove man's accountability and responsibility. The wording of this chapter underscores that God is in absolute control, yet in such a fashion that man is free to follow his own desires while being predestined to do so. Two excellent biblical examples of this are: (1) Genesis 45:4–8; 50:15–21 regarding Joseph's situation; and, (2) Acts 2:22–23 regarding Christ's crucifixion.

Paragraphs three and four begin to narrow down the broad subject of God's decrees by relating it to men and angels. Here, predestination comes into view. God creates men and angels and directs them to their predetermined destiny.

The confession is a double-predestination document, not in any neo-orthodox sense where all are lost in Adam and then all elected in Christ, but in the biblical sense that some men and angels are predestined to everlasting life and some to their lost estate. No other confessional statement that we have read is more forthright in such a position. Predestination is determined solely by God.

Paragraph five narrows the chapter further. While the whole of the chapter makes the application of God's decrees to creation, men, and angels, here begins the application to mankind. We learn first in paragraph five that man's salvation is solely dependent on the grace of God. The gospel of Jesus Christ is a gospel of grace—God doing for us what we cannot do, nor do we deserve. It reminds us that the only condition for our salvation in the final sense is God's electing and saving grace: "Those of mankind that are predestinated unto life, God . . . according to His eternal and immutable purpose, and the secret counsel and good pleasure of his will, hath chosen, in Christ, unto everlasting glory, out of His mere free grace and love."

Paragraph six begins to deal with the specific steps of God's order of salvation. It presents three of man's fourfold states of spiritual existence: (1) "They who are elected," (2) "being fallen in Adam," (3) "are redeemed by Christ," and it spells out the whole plan of salvation from election through sanctification. God is the means and ends of anyone's redemption in Christ Jesus. This paragraph also reminds us that only Christians are saved.

Paragraph seven deals with those among the human race who are not the elect for whom Christ died. They are those for whom Jesus did not die because they were not the elect (see paragraph six). This is where the confession so clearly spells out the double predestination. Those who are not elected are passed by and ordained to dishonor and wrath. Is that unfair of God? Of course not. He passes them by and ordains them to hell "for their sin, to the praise of his glorious justice."

Look at it this way, a person in this category is passed by with saving grace because God wills it. He is ordained to suffer God's wrath because of his sins.

If one understands salvation out of this setting, then he will marvel and praise God for his salvation, for it is only by God's grace that he wasn't passed by and ordained to eternal hell. The confession clearly relates this double predestination to the process of God's unsearchable counsel. Who among us can explain all the details of God's will? None of us. Who among us should marvel and rejoice in his electing grace and redeeming love? All who love God with our hearts, minds, bodies and souls.

The last paragraph issues a warning, and it is most necessary. It is so easy to abuse God's truth and twist it and remove it from the context of his whole counsel. It is a "high mystery." This does not mean that we should not preach it, teach it, and believe. However, it does caution us to be wise and careful in doing so, "that men, attending the will of God revealed in his Word, and yielding obedience thereunto, may . . . be assured of their eternal election." The Bible is God's revealed will, and it teaches us what to believe and how to live. To experience its effectiveness, one must attend to it and yield obedience to it. If properly loved and understood, the doctrine of God's decrees does bring praise, reverence, and admiration for God, and humility, diligence, and abundant consolation to all who sincerely obey the gospel.

Chapter Three ought to remind each Christian that this confession is biblically oriented. It stresses truths that many wish were not so clearly spelled out; yet, faithfulness to Scripture demands that we love all the Word and embrace every doctrine of grace.

Chapter Four
OF CREATION

CONFESSION OF FAITH

1. It pleased God the Father, Son, and Holy Ghost, for the manifestation of the glory of his eternal power, wisdom, and goodness, in the beginning, to create, or make of nothing, the world, and all things therein whether visible or invisible, in the space of six days; and all very good.

2. After God had made all other creatures, he created man, male and female, with reasonable and immortal souls, endued with knowledge, righteousness, and true holiness, after his own image; having the law of God written in their hearts, and power to fulfill it: and yet under a possibility of transgressing, being left to the liberty of their own will, which was subject unto change. Beside this law written in their hearts, they received a command, not to eat of the tree of the knowledge of good and evil; which while they kept, they were happy in their communion with God, and had dominion over the creatures.

WHERE DID WE COME FROM? Is matter eternal? How did what we call creation come about? How long did it take to make it the way it is? Who is responsible? Do the answers to these questions give us any clue as to why we exist and what we are supposed to be doing?

Chapter Four of the Westminster Confession of Faith speaks to the subject of creation or origins with a definite statement of why and for what purpose. If you are teaching this chapter, we suggest a three-point outline such as this: I. The Creator; II. The Creation of the Nonrational; and, III. The Creation of the Rational.

I. The Creator. "In the beginning God created the heavens and the earth" (Gen. 1:1). The first verse of Holy Scripture tells us that the Creator of heaven and earth is God. This is a bold beginning in the modern-day humanistic framework, which seeks to expunge such an idea that God is responsible for creation.

Humanism attempts to deny God's place in regard to his creation, and its best approach is to eliminate him right from the beginning. However, God is our starting point. Only God is eternal. All else is created. Hence the Bible, the only authority in the discussion of origin, and our confession, because it is biblically constructed, begins with the fundamental truth that God is the Creator, not time or chance.

Any view of origins that does not begin with God begins erroneously. Creation did not just happen. God caused it to be. The organic evolution philosophy is wrong in seeking to eliminate God. It opposes the Bible's teaching.

What about theistic evolution, which seeks to explain the present structure of creation by evolutionary process under God's direction? Such a position not only compromises but even contradicts God's testimony. In attempting to synthesize a bit of Scripture with man's unregenerate ideas, one always comes out with untruth.

Who is God? Could God be some impersonal prime moving force without real identity and personality? The only God that the Bible reveals is the Triune God. He is God the Father, God the Son, and God the Holy Spirit. Creation's God is the Triune God.

God the Father, Son, and Holy Spirit created all things. "Then God said, 'Let us make man ...'" (Gen. 1:26). We cannot attribute creation to the work of the Father alone. It was the Father, the Son, and the Holy Spirit.

He took nothing and made from it "the world, and all things therein whether visible or invisible, in the space of six days; and all very good." But why did he do it? Was he incomplete or less a God without creation? Of course not! He did it to reveal the glory of his eternal power, wisdom, and goodness.

If we look at creation properly, we must see the glory of God. It is only the sin factor that keeps us from recognizing him in the visible and invisible parts of creation. Only sin causes us to seek other explanations of our origin.

II. God Created the Nonrational. Genesis 1 gives us the account of God's order of creation. It tells us what he did in creating time and dividing it into days and nights. Step by step, he reveals His orderly fashion of

22

creation. He created matter and formed it into an ordered existence. He then created water and vegetation.

Into that environment of light, water, air, and food, which could then support and sustain animate life, on the fifth day he created the fish, the birds, and the monsters of the sea. On the sixth day, he began to populate the earth with animal life, "according to their kinds."

Order prevailed because God is the Creator who does things decently and in order. All creatures come from God's creative act, and not by some evolutionary chain of life. It is interesting to note that the Genesis record of creation does not begin with microscopic life, as do evolutionary theories.

III. God Created the Rational (Man). "So God created man in his own image, in the image of God he created him; male and female he created them" (Gen. 1:27). God began his human race with one pair, a male and a female, Adam and Eve. Bearing God's image and likeness, man stood in a unique position in creation. For example, God created man with:

- A reasonable soul. He was rational. He could think, talk, dream, and function with personality and individuality. He could put his thoughts into words and talk with God and with other humans. He was not a brute animal, but had a reasonable (rational) life.

- An immortal soul. He was created to live, not die. Though sin later made man subject to death, Jesus Christ came to give eternal life to his own.

- Knowledge, righteousness, and true holiness. Again, we see something of God's likeness in the original man. His capacity for knowledge, righteousness, and true holiness was only reflective of God.

- The likeness and image of God. This is what causes man to stand apart from and above all else in creation. He is the image and likeness of God. He was like God in every way that a creature could be, though man was not nor will ever be God or a god.

23

- God's law written on his heart, with the power to fulfill it or transgress it. Man was made a moral creature to serve the Lord and follow his law, yet he was uniquely made so that he could break God's law and become immoral. God did not make man immoral; he became a sinner by his own choosing. God had made man "very good," but capable of sinning.

- Ability to obey God's law and to have dominion over all of creation. God gave man work to do in ruling over creation as his representative. In order to fulfill his calling, man had to obey God's commands.

While man obeyed, he enjoyed communion with God. He was happy, and he had dominion over all the earth. Chapter Six deals with man's act of disobedience by which he lost his communion with God, his moral uprightness, and his happiness.

When we talk about man today, we cannot do so as though he were still in the original condition in which God made him.

This must be realized in presenting the gospel, attempting to reason with man, or trying to make sense out of his confusion. Man, though like Adam in physical appearance, has been ruined by sin; therefore, he must be born again. He must have his mind, heart, soul, and body renewed after the likeness of Jesus Christ. Without Christ, man is neither good nor capable of carrying out God's creation mandates.

Chapter Five
OF PROVIDENCE

CONFESSION OF FAITH

1. God the great Creator of all things doth uphold, direct, dispose, and govern all creatures, actions, and things, from the greatest even to the least, by his most wise and holy providence, according to his infallible foreknowledge, and the free and immutable counsel of his own will, to the praise of the glory of his wisdom, power, justice, goodness, and mercy.

2. Although, in relation to the foreknowledge and decree of God, the first Cause, all things come to pass immutably, and infallibly; yet, by the same providence, he ordereth them to fall out, according to the nature of second causes, either necessarily, freely, or contingently.

3. God, in his ordinary providence, maketh use of means, yet is free to work without, above, and against them, at his pleasure.

4. The almighty power, unsearchable wisdom, and infinite goodness of God so far manifest themselves in his providence, that it extendeth itself even to the first fall, and all other sins of angels and men; and that not by a bare permission, but such as hath joined with it a most wise and powerful bounding, and otherwise ordering, and governing of them, in a manifold dispensation, to his own holy ends; yet so, as the sinfulness thereof proceedeth only from the creature, and not from God, who, being most holy and righteous, neither is nor can be the author or approver of sin.

5. The most wise, righteous, and gracious God doth oftentimes leave, for a season, his own children to manifold temptations, and the corruption of their own hearts, to chastise them for their former sins, or to discover unto them the hidden strength of corruption and deceitfulness of their hearts, that they may be humbled; and, to raise them to a more close and constant dependence for their support upon himself, and to make them more watchful against all future occasions of sin, and for sundry other just and holy ends.

6. As for those wicked and ungodly men whom God, as a righteous Judge, for former sins, doth blind and harden, from them he not only withholdeth his grace whereby they might have been enlightened in their understandings, and wrought upon in their hearts; but sometimes also withdraweth the gifts which they had, and exposeth them to such objects as their corruption makes occasions of sin; and, withal, gives them over to their own lusts, the temptations of the world, and the power of Satan, whereby it comes to pass that they harden themselves, even under those means which God useth for the softening of others.

7. As the providence of God doth, in general, reach to all creatures; so, after a most special manner, it taketh care of his church, and disposeth all things to the good thereof.

WHAT AN IMPORTANT TRUTH is contained in the doctrine of God's providence! What great comfort and assurance it should bring to those in Christ Jesus! This truth reminds us that God the Creator did not withdraw from his world after he made it, but rather maintains sovereign and personal oversight of its operation. God rules his world and he rules his church.

This doctrine not only gives encouragement to believers in Christ, but also smashes the idea that things happen according to chance, fate, or *luck*. "Whatever will be, will be" may be a popular idea, but the truth is that whatever God wills, will be. The doctrine of providence puts to death the concept of deism, which holds to a belief in a creator god who has withdrawn from his creation and left it to run on its own. It also discards pantheism, which has a god that does rule over and control creation.

The Westminster Confession of Faith divides this doctrine into seven areas to show God's complete control of creation, which implies that God has a relationship with people, events, and nations.

What the confession pulls together systematically from Scripture is the idea that God rules his world. He *ordinarily* does this through means and not by direct intervention; however, he is free to work without means and sometimes does. When he does choose to work without means, he works *extraordinarily*. This is what most people mean today when they use the word "miracle." Because miracles served a particular purpose in the revelation of God during the Old and New Testament periods in the validation of God's Word—a purpose for which we now have Scripture—some people in the Reformed tradition use the term "extraordinary providence" rather than "miracle" in order to reinforce the idea of the sufficiency of Scripture.

When Bible believers use such phraseology, they are not trying to deny his ability in any area. God can and does work ordinarily through means such as consulting physicians and taking medicines, or without means in instantaneous healings, if he so desires.

In our brief space let us look at God's providence from three angles.

First is the teaching of divine preservation. The first paragraph of Chapter Five is probably one of the best summary statements of this teaching, along with Larger Catechism question 18 and Shorter Catechism question 11.

This is God's world. It is not the Devil's. It does not belong to man. God is at the controls. As the sovereign God, he preserves his world. He has that power, wisdom, and concern to sustain his creation moment by moment. "Indeed, he who watches over Israel will neither slumber nor sleep" (Ps. 121:4). There is never a moment when God is not keeping, upholding, empowering, guiding, and directing all of his creation.

The only satisfactory reason that creation still exists is because God is preserving it. He will not allow man to operate autonomously and do anything to his creation that he has not planned. Hebrews 1:3 states that God is "sustaining all things by his powerful word."

A **second** truth taught here and growing out of the first is God's government. God is creator and ruler over his creation. Psalm 97:1: "The LORD reigns, let the earth be glad; let the distant shores rejoice." God directs and rules his world according to his will and purpose, which are of necessity good and perfect.

We need to be reminded of this important truth especially when we are tempted to question God's ways. He always does what is right and in the best interest of all his children. Because he is sovereign, his rule is total. Nothing happens to us, not even sin, outside the will of God. "And we know that in all things God works for the good of those who love him, who

27

have been called according to his purpose" (Rom. 8:28).

To see this we must walk by faith, but that is the essence of the Christian life. "The righteous will live by his faith" (Hab. 2:4). This implies that God rules not only in the big things but also concerning the sparrows of the air, the grass of the field, and the hairs on our heads.

A **third** truth taught in this doctrine is concurrence. Here is the area that separates the Calvinists from the hyper-Calvinists. A true Calvinist, following scriptural revelation, will not fail to see that man is always totally responsible to God for what he does. The hyper-Calvinist, following a rationalistic approach, believes that the sovereignty of God rules out the responsibility of man. But Scripture does not teach this. Man is a responsible creature, and can only be so in light of God's sovereignty. The idea of concurrence brings to mind that the normal or ordinary way that God works in his creation is in a cooperative fashion with all his creatures, in order to cause them to act as he would have them.

Two biblical examples illustrate God's concurrence, working through second causes and thereby making men and angels completely responsible for their actions, yet only to accomplish his will. One is in Genesis 50:20: "You intended to harm me, but God intended it for good to accomplish what is now being done, the saving of many lives." This is a reference to the wicked act of Joseph's brothers in selling Joseph into slavery. They were fully responsible and accountable, yet they served God's purpose.

The other example of concurrence is Jesus' own death, in Acts 2:23: "This man was handed over to you by God's set purpose and foreknowledge; and you, with the help of wicked men, put him to death by nailing him to the cross." The people of Israel did a wicked thing for which they were accountable to God, but they served God's purpose.

Since life and death are in God's hand, a disease may be the immediate cause of a father's death but we know that God is the author of death. God does not ordinarily violate second causes; the way he works is in such a fashion that he is the first cause behind all things that happen, but he is not the cause of evil and iniquity. God does not destroy man's integrity. He allows us to do what we choose to do (within a certain framework) and still accomplishes his purpose, even sin. .

There is great comfort in this deep doctrine. Nothing happens by chance. The Christian can know by faith that he is safe in God's hand. Evil in people and in the world can only go as far as God wills it. As Christians we can live with the truth that while we act and God acts, his actions cause things to work out for good.

Because God is supernatural, he can act as he ordinarily does and accomplish his will through second causes, or he can bypass those second causes and act extraordinarily, without means.

That is the sovereign Lord who loves us who trust Him and commit our lives into his strong hand.

Chapter Six

Of the Fall of Man, of Sin, and of the Punishment Thereof

CONFESSION OF FAITH

1. Our first parents, being seduced by the subtlety and temptation of Satan, sinned, in eating the forbidden fruit. This their sin, God was pleased, according to his wise and holy counsel, to permit, having purposed to order it to his own glory.

2. By this sin they fell from their original righteousness and communion with God, and so became dead in sin, and wholly defiled in all the parts and faculties of soul and body.

3. They being the root of all mankind, the guilt of this sin was imputed; and the same death in sin, and corrupted nature, conveyed to all their posterity descending from them by ordinary generation.

4. From this original corruption, whereby we are utterly indisposed, disabled, and made opposite to all good, and wholly inclined to all evil, do proceed all actual transgressions.

5. This corruption of nature, during this life, doth remain in those that are regenerated; and although it be, through Christ, pardoned, and mortified; yet both itself, and all the motions thereof, are truly and properly sin.

6. Every sin, both original and actual, being a transgression of the righteous law of God, and contrary thereunto, doth, in its own nature, bring guilt upon the sinner, whereby he is bound over to the wrath of God, and curse of the law, and so made subject to death, with all miseries spiritual, temporal, and eternal.

MAN HAS SUCH AN EXALTED opinion of himself that he does not like to think or be reminded that he is a sinner. He tends to think that he is not so bad, and certainly not as bad as he could be. While this kind of attitude is expected in the unbeliever, it is tragic to find those under the umbrella of Christianity who do not want to face the full implications of sin.

You know the type—"Christian ministers" who attempt to convince people to trust in their own goodness, who provocatively suggest that man, the sinner, is not so bad. He may be naughty but he is nice.

The fall of man into sin is a grim reality because it is a contradiction of God's reality. Sin causes death and destruction. God is the author of life. We must be certain that our understanding of the fall of man into sin and the punishment for sin is consistent with God's Word.

Our whole understanding of salvation, with the doctrines of grace and redemption, hinges on a right knowledge and belief about sin. Chapter Six of the Westminster Confession of Faith is most valuable in drawing together the Bible's leaching on the subject of sin.

First, we need to understand that Adam and Eve, the first parents, were real people. They are not symbols for all mankind, but two real people who lived in time and space. Their existence is a matter of history and record— God's history and record. There are many implications of this truth that we must not neglect, especially when considering the organic evolutionary hypothesis. However, for now we shall consider the subject of Chapter Six.

In Chapter Three of the confession, we saw that God ordained sin but was not the author of it. The writers of the confession explained it this way in Chapter Six, 'This their sin, God was pleased, according to His wise and holy counsel, to permit, having purposed to order it to His own glory" (paragraph one).

Is there any difference between God's ordaining sin and God's permitting sin? In the *Institutes of the Christian Religion*, 3.23, John Calvin has some interesting comments on God's will of decree and permission. The reader might refer to that source for some helpful thought.

The confession merely states what Moses indicated in Genesis 3, and Paul in Romans 5, that God permitted our first parents to fall into sin. The statement reminds us that God's purpose behind the fall was his own glory. We must not speculate beyond Scripture, nor may we say something that God does not say.

Let us be concerned with the results of the fall. It has many ramifications; paragraph two mentions several. In the fall, man lost his original righteousness and communion with God. He became dead in sin and wholly defiled in every area of his life.

You may recognize this assessment under the doctrine of total depravity. There is no area of man's life that is not affected by the fall. Now his righteousness is like filthy rags. He no longer personally communes with God. He is dead in sin. All of his faculties are under sin's influence.

Man cannot be acceptable to God on the basis of his goodness, because he has none. Man cannot think or feel in harmony with God's will. He can think and he can feel, but he cannot do so consistent with God's will. He reasons like a fool, as Paul says in Romans 1. He cannot receive the things of the Spirit, as we read in 1 Corinthians 1 and 2. He is totally depraved. He is absolutely dependent on God's revelation, if he is to know the truth.

This has implications in theology, philosophy, arts and sciences, and elsewhere in life. We must not think that fallen man has the same capabilities that he had before he fell. Knowing this will help us understand free will and salvation by grace, which are discussed later in the confession.

Paragraph three reminds us that the sin of our first parents was passed to all their descendants in the human race born by natural or ordinary generation. We have inherited Adam's corrupt nature and are likewise totally depraved. Every man born of woman is a sinner except one, and this is the reason for the confession's wording "descending from them by ordinary generation." Jesus Christ is the exception. He was born of woman, yet supernaturally or by extraordinary generation. He was born without a corrupt nature and was without sin. All other human beings are born dead in trespasses and sin, and in need of the new birth in order to live eternally as children of God.

Paragraph four explains how the original sin with which we are born becomes immediately translated into actual sins. Men do not have to be taught to sin. We come into the world sinning. Sin is as natural to the human race as eating and sleeping. From a corrupt tree comes corrupt fruit. How can one who is totally indisposed, disabled, and made opposite to all good do anything but evil? Of course he cannot help but sin. Man is not neutral. He has an innate disposition to sin. Only a transformation of heart can make him any other way.

That transformation is called "regeneration" or new birth. In paragraph five, the confession is quick to point out that regeneration does change matters. Yet even those born again continue to deal with the corrupt nature. Christians do not cease their sinning when they believe. What they do experience is the pardon of Christ and the mortification of sin (the deadening of bodily appetites and abstinence from sin).

Complete sanctification of life is not ours to experience this side of heaven. There are no sinless people on earth. Christians are not immediately placed in a sinless condition. They live with a corrupt nature until the mortal puts on immortality. Though there may be certain victories over certain sins, there is no final victory until they see the Lord. God's law must always be the schoolmaster, which not only brings man to Christ, but superintends believers as they grow in grace.

What specifically is sin? Paragraph six says that sin, "being a transgression of the righteous law of God, and contrary thereunto, doth in its own nature, bring guilt upon the sinner."

Sin is a most serious matter both for the believer and nonbeliever, maybe more so for the Christian. Christians must love God's law, not transgress it. It displeases God and incurs his wrath for us to sin. It is contrary to our new nature. It is so serious that God indicates that a true believer will not live day after day in sin. Paul asks, "What shall we say, then? Shall we go on sinning so that grace may increase? By no means! We died to sin; how can we live in it any longer?" (Rom. 6:1–2).

For those who have been exposed to the dangerous influences of the higher life, victorious life, or complete sanctification movements, this chapter is so important. B. B. Warfield's *Studies in Perfectionism* is a most important resource book on the subject. Another important book for seeing the Christian life realistically, sins and all, is John Bunyan's *Pilgrim's Progress*.

Christians do sin. "If we claim to be without sin, we deceive ourselves and the truth is not in us" (1 John 1:8). Our hope of forgiveness is in the Lord. Our final hope is in the victory that awaits believers when this earthly pilgrimage is over.

Chapter Seven
OF GOD'S COVENANT WITH MAN

CONFESSION OF FAITH

1. The distance between God and the creature is so great, that although reasonable creatures do owe obedience unto him as their Creator, yet they could never have any fruition of him as their blessedness and reward, but by some voluntary condescension on God's part, which he hath been pleased to express by way of covenant.

2. The first covenant made with man was a covenant of works, wherein life was promised to Adam; and in him to his posterity, upon condition of perfect and personal obedience.

3. Man, by his fall, having made himself incapable of life by that covenant, the Lord was pleased to make a second, commonly called the covenant of grace; wherein he freely offereth unto sinners life and salvation by Jesus Christ; requiring of them faith in him, that they may be saved, and promising to give unto all those that are ordained unto eternal life his Holy Spirit, to make them willing, and able to believe.

4. This covenant of grace is frequently set forth in Scripture by the name of a testament, in reference to the death of Jesus Christ the Testator, and to the everlasting inheritance, with all things belonging to it, therein bequeathed.

5. This covenant was differently administered in the time of the law, and in the time of the gospel: under the law, it was administered by promises, prophecies, sacrifices, circumcision, the paschal lamb, and other types and ordinances delivered to the people of the Jews, all foresignifying Christ to come; which were, for that time, sufficient and efficacious, through the operation of the Spirit, to instruct and build up the elect in faith in the promised Messiah, by whom they had full remission of sins, and eternal salvation; and is called the old testament.

6. Under the gospel, when Christ, the substance, was exhibited, the ordinances

in which this covenant is dispensed are the preaching of the Word, and the administration of the sacraments of baptism and the Lord's Supper: which, though fewer in number, and administered with more simplicity, and less outward glory, yet, in them, it is held forth in more fullness, evidence and spiritual efficacy, to all nations, both Jews and Gentiles; and is called the new testament. There are not therefore two covenants of grace, differing in substance, but one and the same, under various dispensations.

PRIOR TO THIS subject of covenant truth, the Westminster Confession of Faith has dealt with the foundational doctrines of the Christian faith—Scripture, God, Decrees, Creation, Providence, and Sin. Remove these truths from Christianity and the entire faith collapses. Actually, the doctrines of the faith, set forth in Scripture, stand or fall together; they form a system.

One could say that each doctrine taught in Scripture is foundational; yet as we approach the subject in Chapter Seven—God's Covenant with Man—it would help to think of the covenant as the heart of Christianity. The Covenant of Grace is the focal point of the Christian faith. Basically, it states, "I will be your God and the God of your children." This truth puts flesh on the reality of God's electing grace, plus it gives impetus to the evangelistic message.

Let us use these six paragraphs to highlight this central truth. First we need to ask, What is a covenant? Often one hears it said that a covenant is an agreement between one or more parties. This suggests that God and man come together and set up a covenant, and by that contract or testament they relate to one another. One could easily infer as much, especially from the Child's Catechism and faulty biblical interpretation.

As we read paragraph one, we learn that such an idea is absurd. It reminds us that God is the Creator, and we are the creatures. It is only by God's voluntary condescension that God and man can come together. We cannot go to God, but he can and does come to us, and we relate to him by way of a covenant.

Understand man's role in the covenant contract: we hear God's terms, i.e., we read his will and either accept it obediently or reject it. The terms are God's, the conditions are his, and the requirement is our full obedience.

God negotiated his own covenant. He set the terms, and he took the initiative. We must follow with submissive obedience. If man's responsibility is to obey God's will, does this suggest that God has violated man's free will or choice? No, there is no "free" will in sinful man in the full sense of the term.

This cuts across the grain of modern man, who has been programmed to believe that he rather than God is sovereign and free. This is a matter of humanism vs. belief in the personal God, the battle raging in our culture.

This chapter also explains that God's covenant with man, which grows out of his eternal counsel, has two parts: the covenant of works and the covenant of grace. We learn here that the covenant of grace has experienced two types of administration.

What is the covenant of works? Paragraph two defines it as a covenant "wherein life was promised to Adam; and in him to his posterity, upon condition of perfect and personal obedience." Some call this the "covenant of life." This covenant dealt with God's relation to man through Adam. It made clear that though man enjoyed a sweet communion with God, it was a time of probation. Adam's test for himself and his posterity was to obey God's covenant of works. We read of this in Genesis 2, especially in verses 9 and 15–17.

We are reminded in paragraph three of Chapter Seven of the grim reality that Adam broke God's covenant. He disobeyed. He lost his capacity to please God. In Adam we all have sinned and lost our ability to please God. The covenant of works that originally was a signpost to life is now by itself a road to death.

Now it is interesting and humbling to realize that because God's covenants are eternal, the covenant of works still stands and offers life to perfectly obedient human beings. The problem is that there are none righteous and capable of earning eternal life.

Does this suggest that God is playing some kind of game of Russian roulette with us? Of course not! "The Lord was pleased to make a second, commonly called the covenant of grace; wherein He freely offereth unto sinners life and salvation by Jesus Christ; requiring of them faith in Him, that they may be saved, and promising to give unto all those that are ordained unto life His Holy Spirit, to make them willing, and able to believe," we read in paragraph three. This is the gospel in a nutshell. It is how and only how God's promise to be our God and to grant to us eternal life can be realized.

The gospel would not be good news unless it spoke of what God has done to save us who could never save ourselves, or God doing for us what we do not deserve nor are we capable of doing. The gospel is always presented in covenantal form.

As the gospel of God's grace is proclaimed, his covenant conditions must be underscored. To be saved by Christ, to know God as our God and the God of our children, he requires of us faith in him. By his Holy Spirit's working in our lives in what we call the new birth, God makes us capable of trusting Him.

For that reason, as we shall observe in detail in future chapters, faith in Christ cannot precede the new birth. The new birth (regeneration) must take place before one can be converted to Christ. By the grace of God, those ordained to eternal life continue to believe into life everlasting.

No man has ever been saved apart from the covenant of grace, for man is saved only by grace through faith (Eph. 2:8–9). The covenant of grace was operative in Old Testament times and was expressed in the law and administered by promises, prophecies, sacrifices, and other means (paragraph five). People were saved then by their faith in the hope that God would redeem them by his grace.

When the gospel was fulfilled in New Testament times, the promise and deliverance were one and the same as in the Old Testament, except Christ had come. We are saved by faith in that same hope and fulfillment as were our fathers in the Old Testament times.

Let no man proclaim to you that salvation has ever been accomplished any other way. Since the Garden of Eden, the seed of the woman introduced in Genesis 3:15—whom we now know as Jesus Christ—has been the only Savior of sinners. Every soul in heaven today has gone there by hope in the Deliverer (Jesus Christ). There is no other way.

The true church is established around this doctrine of covenant redemption. God is the sovereign Creator and Redeemer of his people. We are saved because of him and his grace. His condition for salvation must be expounded and believed. Man must ever be impressed with the absolute necessity of faith in Jesus Christ alone for eternal life.

The heart of the Christian faith is God's covenant of grace with man. Let us be careful not to share its place with any other idea. "I will be your God and the God of your children," but only by grace. Hear this in preaching. See it visible in the sacraments of baptism and the Lord's Supper. Enjoy it through communion with God (paragraph six).

Chapter Eight

Of Christ the Mediator

Confession of Faith

1. It pleased God, in his eternal purpose, to choose and ordain the Lord Jesus, his only begotten Son, to be the Mediator between God and man, the Prophet, Priest, and King, the Head and Savior of his church, the Heir of all things, and Judge of the world: unto whom he did from all eternity give a people, to be his seed, and to be by him in time redeemed, called, justified, sanctified, and glorified.

2. The Son of God, the second person in the Trinity, being very and eternal God, of one substance and equal with the Father, did, when the fullness of time was come, take upon him man's nature, with all the essential properties, and common infirmities thereof, yet without sin; being conceived by the power of the Holy Ghost, in the womb of the virgin Mary, of her substance. So that two whole, perfect, and distinct natures, the Godhead and the manhood, were inseparably joined together in one person, without conversion, composition, or confusion. Which person is very God, and very man, yet one Christ, the only Mediator between God and man.

3. The Lord Jesus, in his human nature thus united to the divine, was sanctified, and anointed with the Holy Spirit, above measure, having in him all the treasures of wisdom and knowledge; in whom it pleased the Father that all fullness should dwell; to the end that, being holy, harmless, undefiled, and full of grace and truth, he might be thoroughly furnished to execute the office of a mediator, and surety. Which office he took not unto himself, but was thereunto called by his Father, who put all power and judgment into his hand, and gave him commandment to execute the same.

4. This office the Lord Jesus did most willingly undertake; which that he might discharge, he was made under the law, and did perfectly fulfill it; endured most grievous torments immediately in his soul, and most painful sufferings in his body; was crucified, and died, was buried, and remained under the power of death, yet saw no corruption. On the third day he arose from the

dead, with the same body in which he suffered, with which also he ascended into heaven, and there sitteth at the right hand of his Father, making intercession, and shall return, to judge men and angels, at the end of the world.

5.   The Lord Jesus, by his perfect obedience, and sacrifice of himself, which he, through the eternal Spirit, once offered up unto God, hath fully satisfied the justice of his Father; and purchased, not only reconciliation, but an everlasting inheritance in the kingdom of heaven, for all those whom the Father hath given unto him.

6.   Although the work of redemption was not actually wrought by Christ till after his incarnation, yet the virtue, efficacy, and benefits thereof were communicated unto the elect, in all ages successively from the beginning of the world, in and by those promises, types, and sacrifices, wherein he was revealed, and signified to be the seed of the woman which should bruise the serpent's head; and the Lamb slain from the beginning of the world; being yesterday and today the same, and forever.

7.   Christ, in the work of mediation, acts according to both natures, by each nature doing that which is proper to itself; yet, by reason of the unity of the person, that which is proper to one nature is sometimes in Scripture attributed to the person denominated by the other nature.

8.   To all those for whom Christ hath purchased redemption, he doth certainly and effectually apply and communicate the same; making intercession for them, and revealing unto them, in and by the Word, the mysteries of salvation; effectually persuading them by his Spirit to believe and obey, and governing their hearts by his Word and Spirit; overcoming all their enemies by his almighty power and wisdom, in such manner, and ways, as are most consonant to his wonderful and unsearchable dispensation.

THIS CHAPTER in the Westminster Confession of Faith is crucial. It contains truth that is absolutely essential to the reality and preservation of the Christian faith because it deals with the doctrine on which our redemption stands, namely, Jesus Christ the Mediator between God and man.

Down through the history of the church, both in the Old and New Testament eras, men have debated the person and work of the Messiah. Some Jews of Old Testament times were not certain as to his person and work. Was he to be a champion leader of the Jewish people for human rights, or would he be God to redeem his people from sin?

When Christ Jesus was on the earth, there was continuous debate as to his identity. This type of inquiry and speculation has not ceased to this day. Chapter Eight draws together masterfully from God's Word, Genesis to Revelation, and takes into consideration all the objections and conclusions made by men regarding the person of the Lord Jesus Christ down through history.

We shall discuss truth in three areas: **first**, the person of Christ; **second**, the office of Christ; and **third**, the work of Christ. If you are teaching this chapter, you could follow this basic division.

The person of Christ deals with who Jesus Christ is. To orthodox Christians, the answer is simple because we walk by faith in God's Word, which tells us who he is. Yet men have not always understood nor accepted the Bible's teaching. You would find sections of early church history most interesting and informative, especially in those areas dealing with the formulation of the Christian doctrines. One popular church history book is by B. K. Kuiper, *The Church in History*. Chapter Five of that book contains an excellent summation of the heresies and affirmations concerning the person of Christ.

What kind of person was Jesus of Nazareth? Was he a person with God-like characteristics? Was he perhaps not fully God, yet first among created beings? Was he totally God disguised as a man?

Paragraphs one, two, and three answer these questions. Jesus was totally God. He was everything that God is. He lacked nothing in deity. Also, he was totally human. With the exception of sin, he was everything that man is. The amazing truth is that he is the God-Man, one person with two distinct natures, inseparably joined in his incarnation.

On this truth hinges the entire redemption of the church. The early church councils stood firmly on this affirmation that Jesus Christ is fully divine and fully human. It is the spirit of the antichrist that denies this identity of Jesus (1 John 4:2–3). Christians believe that Jesus is one person with two natures, human and divine.

The *office of Christ* is that of Mediator. Yet we speak of that office in three areas—prophet, priest, and king. God had made man to be prophet, priest, and king, but sin kept man from fulfilling his office. As the Mediator between God and his people, Christ was the perfect prophet, priest, and king.

As the Prophet, Christ brought God's message to man. Even before his virgin birth, he acted as prophet by being the Angel of the Lord in the Old Testament, and by working in and through the Old Testament prophets.

In his incarnate state, Christ was the prophet on earth. He proclaimed God's message to man. He continues as the prophet through his Word and Spirit. In the preaching of his Word and the illumination of believers, Jesus speaks God's Word to man. He had to be God to be the perfect prophet of God.

As the Priest, Christ represents the church before God. He is a "priest forever in the order of Melchizedek" (Heb. 7:17). The priest, according to Scripture, must be a man who represents his people, but one especially appointed by the Lord. He offers the sacrifice for man's sin. He also prays for his people.

Jesus was the perfect priest who went into God's presence on behalf of his people, offering his own blood as the atonement for their sins and interceding for them. He had to be a man completely consecrated to God. If Jesus had been only somewhat like man, he could not have fulfilled his office of priest. He was the perfect man.

The Old Testament priestly system, with its sacrificial rites and intercessory functions, all pointed to him who was the complete priest.

As the King, Christ rules and reigns over his creation. He is the unique king and head of the church, and he is also the king of creation. As the king of the church, his rule is a spiritual one. By means of the Word and the Spirit, he exercises his kingship.

He also has all authority over heaven and earth. He rules the world. The universe does not belong to Satan, but is God's world. Christ, as God, rules his world. He guides the destiny of men and nations. We must remember that the church belongs to him, and must submit to his will. The world must also submit to him and obey his will.

As the God-Man, Christ is the perfect Prophet, Priest, and King. His role of Mediator between God and man is perfectly carried out. Nothing is lacking.

The last area is the work of Christ. His work could be summarized this way: God the Father chose and ordained him and gave him a particular people. For them he was to be the perfect sacrifice. He was to die on their behalf and in their place. Those represented by Christ at the cross would in time be redeemed, called, justified, sanctified, and glorified (paragraph one).

This is the good news of the gospel in capsule form: that God by his Son Jesus has accomplished redemption for his people, and by his grace through the proclamation of the Word he will "certainly and effectively apply and communicate the same . . ." (paragraph eight).

His work as Mediator and Redeemer was for the elect, the people chosen by God and given to his Son. He represented God before his people, and he represents his people before God.

The good news is not centered on man and what he must do to be saved, but rather on Jesus Christ who by his perfect work saves sinners. "Christ died for the ungodly" (Rom. 5:6). He suffered entirely for his own.

We must learn from his Word who he is and what he does. It is by the Word that the Holy Spirit persuades those for whom Jesus died to believe and obey Jesus Christ.

Christ the Mediator does not deal with possibilities, but rather actualities. He did not simply make salvation possible. He actually secured it. He died for what the angel Gabriel told the Virgin Mary he would do. "She will give birth to a son, and you are to give him the name Jesus, because he will save his people from their sins" (Matt. 1:21).

Chapter Nine
OF FREE WILL

CONFESSION OF FAITH

1. God hath endued the will of man with that natural liberty, that it is neither forced, nor, by any absolute necessity of nature, determined to good, or evil.

2. Man, in his state of innocency, had freedom, and power to will and to do that which was good and well pleasing to God; but yet, mutably, so that he might fall from it.

3. Man, by his fall into a state of sin, hath wholly lost all ability of will to any spiritual good accompanying salvation: so as, a natural man, being altogether averse from that good, and dead in sin, is not able, by his own strength, to convert himself, or to prepare himself thereunto.

4. When God converts a sinner, and translates him into the state of grace, he freeth him from his natural bondage under sin; and, by his grace alone, enables him freely to will and to do that which is spiritually good; yet so, as that by reason of his remaining corruption, he doth not perfectly, nor only, will that which is good, but doth also will that which is evil.

5. The will of man is made perfectly and immutably free to good alone, in the state of glory only.

WE HAVE COME across people in our travels and ministries who have varied backgrounds with diverse understandings. One of the most obvious problems within the Christian framework is the doctrinal system known as Calvinism. People are either very positive or very negative with respect to the Calvinistic view of Christianity.

More times than not, we find that negative attitudes toward Calvinism, or Presbyterianism, grow out of misunderstanding or because overly enthusiastic individuals misapply it and thereby cause somewhat of a distortion.

This chapter addresses one of the major areas that have generated negative attitudes—the free will of man. We know that some reject the Calvinistic approach to theology simply because it does not teach that man has free will; hence, they believe he cannot be held responsible. How many people have you heard make such a statement?

In reality, what many people reject is not Calvinism/Presbyterianism but rather a misunderstanding or misapplication of it. For example, those who talk about man in a totally deterministic or fatalistic manner, saying that man is not free and responsible under Calvinism, are not talking about any Presbyterian doctrine at all, but rather a type of hyper-Calvinism.

Hyper-Calvinism is a scholastic approach that often is held to say, "If I cannot harmonize two areas of thought, I must reject one of those areas." The resulting hyper-Calvinist position is one that rejects human freedom and responsibility.

Does this mean that the opposite extreme, held by the Arminian tradition, is consistently biblical when it emphasizes the freedom/responsibility aspect of Christianity while being silent on the sovereignty of God? Of course not. The consistently biblical position emphasizes both God's sovereignty and human responsibility.

The Bible teaches that God is sovereign and determines all things that come to pass, even man's eternity. Remember our study in Chapter Three? However, the Bible also teaches that man was created with free will and is responsible to God for everything he says and does.

The free will of man is a point of contention with diverse aspects, and has caused much debate through the centuries. As far back as the fifth century, free will was the issue in debates between the forces of Augustine and those of Pelagius: "Does man have free will?"

While space here does not permit a detailed summary of the issue of free will, the serious student could pursue books such as *Freedom of the Will* by Jonathan Edwards and *Bondage of the Will* by Martin Luther. Below are several general comments, and then specific remarks on Chapter Nine of the Westminster Confession.

First, man normally is not a "machine" in his behavior. While at times he allows himself to be manipulated or controlled, he usually makes decisions about almost everything. Unless he is drugged, shocked, or psychologically programmed, he makes conscious choices that affect his words, deeds, and direction. Behaviorists such as B. F. Skinner are at odds with biblical truth when they see man as being programmed or controlled by his environment. Man makes choices and decisions. He is no fatalist.

Second, when we refer to freedom of the will, we are talking about liberty and not ability. This is an important distinction. Liberty and ability are not synonymous. People have liberty to do what they wish, but this does not mean they have the ability.

Third, the idea that man has free will must be viewed with the understanding that man today is not the same man morally that God made him to be. We saw this in Chapter Six when we looked at man's fall into sin.

The Confession of Faith is brilliantly developed in all areas, and Chapter Nine is no exception. In these brief paragraphs, we have a progression that follows the chronological revelation of Scripture and gives us the whole story regarding man's freedom of the will.

One confuses reality when he tries, apart from these truths, to understand man's condition and needs. This comes into view when we look at humanism. All persons are responsible to choose God and accountable if they reject him, and even those who reject God cannot live and act outside the realm of a moral environment. Man is not the sole determiner of his life, nor is he in complete control of it. Christians do not believe that man is autonomous.

What does the Bible teach? First, it shows us man as God made him. Originally, man was made in God's image and likeness. God "endued the will of man with that natural liberty . . ." (paragraph one). With that liberty, man has the ability to do good and to choose good without any outside force working on him. As paragraph two states: "Man, in his state of innocency, had freedom, and power to will and to do that which was good and well pleasing to God; but yet, mutably, so that he might fall from it."

He could choose good or he could choose evil. God made him that way originally. What did he do? He chose evil.

Then what? It is at this point we are reminded that we cannot deal with man today as God made him, but rather as he is ruined by sin. How did sin ruin man? Did it destroy his person? No, but sin did cause man to lose his ability to choose to do anything acceptable in God's sight. Sin caused him to be "altogether averse from that good, and dead in sin, . . . not able, by his own strength, to convert himself, or to prepare himself thereunto" (paragraph three).

Apart from the new birth (regeneration), man cannot do anything morally pleasing and acceptable to God. His will is no longer free because, in his fallen state, he cannot please God nor will to do God's will. He is a slave to sin. Scripture is full of such references about man (Rom. 3:10, 12; 5:6; John 15:5b). How can a man in this condition be told that he must believe or have faith in order to be born again? If such were possible, the new birth would be superfluous. Man, the sinner, does not have free will in moral areas. He is a slave to sin. If he did have free will, it would mean at most that he had the liberty to please God but not the ability, because of the fall into sin.

Continuing with God's plan, the confession in paragraph four makes it clear that God does not leave man in bondage to sin. When God redeems him, he "freeth him from his natural bondage under sin; and, by His grace alone, enables him freely to will and to do that which is spiritually good . . . ."

The new birth, reaching its expression in conversion, restores and thus enables one to choose to do God's will. It is dangerous and misleading to teach that, prior to the new birth, man can have saving faith or do any good in God's sight. The only way for him to work out his salvation is for God to work in him (Phil. 2:13).

Paragraph five states, "The will of man is made perfectly and immutably free to do good alone in the state of glory only." Complete freedom of the will from evil is only available when we are with the Lord in heaven. Till that time we must struggle with God's will. Though the Christian now has both the liberty and the ability, he is not yet free from sin.

Therefore, while on the one hand we can talk about a Christian having free will because of his new birth in Christ, coming to expression in his conversion, we must also remember that perfect freedom to serve God is part of the final victory that shall be ours as we go to be with the Lord in glory.

The contents of Chapter Nine will enable one to keep his focus on man's true perspective and situation. It will keep him from any delusions of grandeur. It will cause him to glory in the Lord who has freed him from bondage to sin and enabled him to will to do the will of God.

Chapter Ten

OF EFFECTUAL CALLING

CONFESSION OF FAITH

1. All those whom God hath predestinated unto life, and those only, he is pleased, in his appointed and accepted time, effectually to call, by his Word and Spirit, out of that state of sin and death, in which they are by nature, to grace and salvation, by Jesus Christ; enlightening their minds spiritually and savingly to understand the things of God, taking away their heart of stone, and giving unto them a heart of flesh; renewing their wills, and, by his almighty power, determining them to that which is good, and effectually drawing them to Jesus Christ: yet so, as they come most freely, being made willing by his grace.

2. This effectual call is of God's free and special grace alone, not from anything at all foreseen in man, who is altogether passive therein, until, being quickened and renewed by the Holy Spirit, he is thereby enabled to answer this call, and to embrace the grace offered and conveyed in it.

3. Elect infants, dying in infancy, are regenerated, and saved by Christ, through the Spirit, who worketh when, and where, and how he pleaseth: so also are all other elect persons who are incapable of being outwardly called by the ministry of the Word.

4. Others, not elected, although they may be called by the ministry of the Word, and may have some common operations of the Spirit, yet they never truly come unto Christ, and therefore cannot be saved: much less can men, not professing the Christian religion, be saved in any other way whatsoever, be they never so diligent to frame their lives according to the light of nature, and the laws of that religion they do profess. And, to assert and maintain that they may, is very pernicious, and to be detested.

CHAPTER TEN begins the section of the Confession of Faith that sets forth the *ordo salutis*, i.e., the order of salvation or redemption accomplished and applied.

It is important that Christians have a faith that is built on an understanding of Scripture. We do not have to know everything in Scripture in order to be saved, but God has been pleased to reveal in his Word those things that He would have us know and understand for salvation. We make no dichotomy between faith and knowledge, as did disciples of the Greek gods, though we point to the primacy of faith. "We believe in order to understand" is the Christian's motto. Or as Anselm of Canterbury wrote in the eleventh century: "I do not seek to understand that I may believe, but I believe in order to understand. For this I believe—that unless I believe, I should not understand."

This chapter begins to explain how sinners embrace the saving grace of God offered in Christ. It explains how a spiritually dead person can respond to the gospel; how one can hear and embrace and another can hear and reject; and how we can hope that certain infants dying in infancy are saved.

Have you ever wondered why you trusted Jesus Christ? What moved you to that point? Was it a mere personal whim that led you to confess Jesus? Did you say you believed because you had a sudden feeling or urge? Such questions are good ones because, if we listen to Scripture's answers, it will help us to understand a most vital part of salvation. Let us establish several ground rules in order to consider this subject. **First**, though some have said that the gospel call is not universal, we maintain that it is a worldwide call to be offered to and impressed on all men. Jesus' commission to go into all the world is our mandate. **Second**, though we know that "many are called but few are chosen" and though we have no right to pass prior judgment on a man's election, we must urgently and sincerely call men to faith and repentance. **Third**, though God is the author of the gospel call, he normally works through men to accomplish his task; we have an evangelistic imperative placed on us. **Fourth**, we must be careful in presenting the gospel and inviting men to Christ so that we not mislead them about how this happens.

The first paragraph simply states that God predestines men to eternal life. It also says that in order to be saved, a man must "spiritually and savingly . . . understand the things of God . . . [to] come most freely" to

Christ. But how can that be? we ask.

We know that apart from Christ we are dead in trespasses and sin. How can a dead man have spiritual understanding? How can he come freely to Jesus Christ? Is he not really dead after all?

The Scriptures and our Westminster Standards appear to make a distinction within the call of the gospel between the outward call that many hear and the inward call that brings the elect to life. It works like this: as the gospel is proclaimed, God is pleased in his own time to speak to that person's heart; we could call this the new birth, or at least say that the inward call begins the process of the new birth. God calls the sinner from death to life, from darkness to light, from unbelief to faith. He changes the hearts of stone to hearts of flesh, and for the first time the sinner sees the truth and embraces the gospel of Jesus Christ.

This is how a person can be rebellious and hard toward God, but let God speak to that person inwardly, and he is converted. This is how the Westminster Confession can say that no one comes to Christ except freely and willingly. God works in the sinner's heart and makes him willing to come to saving faith. The timing of one's response is in God's hand.

We cannot presume that God is inwardly calling men every time we preach the Word publicly or privately, so we must be careful not to mislead man to believe that he can come to Christ at his own pleasure. However, we must constantly present the gospel to all men, urging them to trust in Jesus Christ, to accept him by faith, in order to obtain the forgiveness of sin and eternal life. We must present the gospel truths. There must be an invitation to accept Christ in faith and repentance, and there must be the promise of forgiveness and salvation to all who believe and repent, always remembering that one can only come if Jesus Christ, by his Word and Spirit, effectually calls.

One can easily see that when this process is understood, the preacher, the personal witness, and the sinner can point only to God's grace in one's salvation. Coupled with the truth of paragraph two that the inward call of the gospel does not come to a person because he has anything in himself that commends him to God, and acknowledging that to this point the sinner is altogether passive, we see that salvation is completely from God. Only by the grace of God can a person answer the call of the gospel.

Paragraph four explains this even further when it states that men can hear the gospel, have some common operations of the Holy Spirit, and yet never truly come to Christ. What makes the difference is the eternal call of God by his Word and Spirit. Those who hear the gospel and do not accept it are not saved. No person, no matter how religious outwardly or inwardly, has eternal life unless his religious experience grows out of a saving relationship to Jesus Christ. "Salvation is found in no one else, for there is no other name under heaven given to men by which we must be saved" (Acts 4:12).

But what about those who die in infancy? If a person cannot be saved without accepting Christ, does that mean that babies who die are lost?

That is an interesting question and one filled with great emotional overtones. Christians are free to speak only what Scripture says on such matters, not their own opinions. However, Scripture does offer some help here, and paragraph three is a good, concise response to the question. We believe that elect infants, or any elect persons who die before they can make a profession of faith, are regenerated and saved.

Jesus indicated in Luke 18:15–16 that tiny children are part of the kingdom of God. God said, "I will be your God and the God of your children."

Again the emphasis here as with man's acceptance of the gospel is directed toward God and his grace. That is where it belongs. It is neither trite nor counterproductive to have this theological understanding of God's plan of redemption. People without this understanding have often presented the gospel as though salvation is completely dependent on man. Instead of God being faithfully set forth as the only Savior of sinners, he is often seen as a co-savior with man.

If these are biblical truths, and we believe they are or they would not be part of our confessional position, we must hold to them in order to preach God's Word truthfully and faithfully. We must preach the gospel and call men to Christ, but in a biblical manner. We must not be timid in presenting the gospel and urging men to repent and believe, offering the promise of forgiveness and life to all who do. Our prayer is that as we present the gospel of Christ that "all who were appointed for eternal life believed" (Acts 13:48).

Chapter Eleven

Of Justification

Confession of Faith

1.   Those whom God effectually calleth, he also freely justifieth: not by infusing righteousness into them, but by pardoning their sins, and by accounting and accepting their persons as righteous; not for anything wrought in them, or done by them, but for Christ's sake alone; nor by imputing faith itself, the act of believing, or any other evangelical obedience to them, as their righteousness; but by imputing the obedience and satisfaction of Christ unto them, they receiving and resting on him and his righteousness, by faith; which faith they have not of themselves, it is the gift of God.

2.   Faith, thus receiving and resting on Christ and his righteousness, is the alone instrument of justification: yet is it not alone in the person justified, but is ever accompanied with all other saving graces, and is no dead faith, but worketh by love.

3.   Christ, by his obedience and death, did fully discharge the debt of all those that are thus justified, and did make a proper, real, and full satisfaction to his Father's justice in their behalf. Yet, inasmuch as he was given by the Father for them; and his obedience and satisfaction accepted in their stead; and both, freely, not for anything in them; their justification is only of free grace; that both the exact justice and rich grace of God might be glorified in the justification of sinners.

4.   God did, from all eternity, decree to justify all the elect, and Christ did, in the fullness of time, die for their sins, and rise again for their justification: nevertheless, they are not justified, until the Holy Spirit doth, in due time, actually apply Christ unto them.

5.   God doth continue to forgive the sins of those that are justified; and, although they can never fall from the state of justification, yet they may, by their sins, fall under God's fatherly displeasure, and not have the light of his countenance restored unto them, until they humble themselves, confess their

sins, beg pardon, and renew their faith and repentance.

6. The justification of believers under the old testament was, in all these respects, one and the same with the justification of believers under the new testament.

HOW DOES GOD accept guilty sinners into his kingdom? How can sinful man ever hope to stand before a righteous God? A simplistic answer is that a person who has faith in Christ can on that basis stand before the righteous God. This is generally true, but the precise biblical response is that we can stand before God because Jesus Christ has justified us. He has satisfied God's wrath and accomplished our pardon by his saving grace alone.

How can we ever hope to be saved and go to heaven? The only answer is because Jesus Christ by his obedience and satisfaction to God on our behalf has justified us (pardoned our sins), thus enabling us to stand before the holy God in Christ's righteousness.

This chapter of the Westminster Confession of Faith contains another essential teaching in the gospel of Jesus—"Of Justification"— another link in God's golden chain of salvation. It is extremely important for all believers to have an understanding of this doctrine in order to have assurance of salvation.

As we shall observe in Chapter Seventeen, assurance of salvation is not essential for someone to be saved. Many Christians live without assurance that they are redeemed. In *Pilgrim's Progress,* Pilgrim comes to the wicket gate and enters, thus symbolizing his conversion to Christ. He keeps his burden of sin until he comes to the cross, symbolizing his understanding of what happened at Calvary and thus understanding his justification. Only then does his burden fall from him into the pit.

If one believes the whole biblical teaching on justification, it will encourage and assure him that in Christ Jesus, he can stand in the Holy God's presence and not be condemned.

Paul writes in Romans 5:1, "Therefore, since we have been justified through faith, we have peace with God through our Lord Jesus Christ." Justification, properly understood and applied, brings peace with God and inner peace for those who know the Lord as their justifier.

Four main aspects of this crucial doctrine are set forth in six paragraphs of Chapter Eleven. **First**, the elect of God are justified in Christ. **Second**, Christ merits our justification and we are the benefactors by faith in him. **Third**, Jesus Christ paid our sin debt to God, thereby giving us pardon from God. **Fourth**, all believers of both testament periods experience the same justification.

First, paragraph four states God decreed to justify the elect on the basis of Jesus Christ's work at the cross. On the one hand, Christians are spoken of as believers who have been justified from all eternity. However, it must be clearly understood that though God decreed the justification of believers, they were not in fact justified until Jesus died and rose again from the grave, or more specifically, "They are not justified, until the Holy Spirit doth, in due time, actually apply Christ unto them."

Though God foreordains the pardon of the elect, it does not happen in reality until the Holy Spirit works savingly in an individual's life. So we must not equate God's decree to justify us with our actual pardon, though justification grows out of God's decree.

Understanding this distinction will enable us to know that our only hope and plea is in Christ alone, and that he took our sins on himself to work out or accomplish our pardon.

Second, the confession reminds us that Jesus Christ alone paid for our sins, and by faith in him we receive the benefits of pardon. Paragraph two contains a crucial aspect to this doctrine. It points out two extremely important lessons. The first lesson is that "Faith. thus receiving and resting on Christ and his righteousness, is the alone instrument of justification . . . ." Christ alone is the ground of our acceptance by God. We can't offer our works, our talents, our material possessions, or our educational achievements. All we can do is trust in Christ alone. As the hymn writer stated it, "Nothing in my hands I bring, simply to thy cross I cling." Faith is dependence on Christ to do for us what we would not and could not do for ourselves. This idea expels any notions of earning our justification, or making ourselves acceptable in God's sight, or meriting his favor. Christ alone is our hope. The second lesson under point two reminds us that while faith in Christ alone is the only way to be justified, such faith ". . . is no dead faith, but worketh by love."

While we are not justified by works or any other saving grace, we are not justified without them either. They are the heads and tails of the same coin. James could therefore say, "faith without deeds is dead" (James 2:26b). Good works are a sign of saving faith and justification.

We must know that Christians, truly trusting in Christ alone for redemption, will bear fruit. Their faith will be accompanied by works, but this does not indicate that good works are part of the plan of meriting God's favor in order that an individual might be justified. If we could relate this to time it would be like this: we must trust Christ alone but, as we trust him, that faith begins to reveal itself by the accompanying saving grace. A genuine saving faith does produce good works. While the root of justification is faith in Christ alone, the faith produces not only our pardon from sins but also the evidence of good works in our lives. Justification pardons us not so we might continue in sin, but so we might live like true children of God.

Third, the Confession of Faith is clear in underscoring that Christ paid the debt for sin. God's anger and wrath because of our sins can only be removed by the saving work of Christ. The greatness of sin's debt could only be paid by the magnitude of Christ's death. Paragraph three states, "Christ, by His obedience and death, did fully discharge the debt of all those that are thus justified . . . ." A person's only hope for forgiveness for all sins past, present, and future is Jesus' satisfactory payment for all our sins.

The Westminster Confession reminds us that because Jesus was faithful and obedient until death, the Father's divine justice is satisfied. God was satisfied not because we stopped sinning suddenly; but because Jesus paid it all. He is a complete and perfect Savior.

Fourth, paragraph four of Chapter Eleven reminds us that believers of both Old Testament and New Testament times, on both sides of the cross (BC and AD), receive the same justification. There is not nor has there ever been any other way for a sinner to stand before the holy God than in the righteousness of Christ alone. The Old Testament believers were not justified by the works of the law any more than New Testament believers are. Faith in the promised Deliverer was the key to the Old Testament believers' acceptance by God. Faith in the fulfillment of the promise of the Savior is the ground of the New Testament believers' pardon and acceptance.

This is important especially in light of the Dispensational school of thought, which teaches that God has worked savingly in different ways at different times in history. At all times since the fall there has been only one Redeemer, one justifier of sinful man, Jesus Christ. He alone is able "to save to the uttermost." We are not justified because we have kept God's law. We are justified because Christ alone kept God's law perfectly and took our sins upon his body on the tree. Nevertheless, the justified have the privilege and obligation to keep the law of God.

We are not justified by sanctification but justification is the key to our sanctification. "Shall we go on sinning so that grace may increase? By no means! We died to sin; how can we live in it any longer?" (Rom. 6:1b–2).

Because several prominent schools of thought besides Dispensationalism are at odds with this doctrine, it would be good for Christians to study this doctrine well. Suggested reference books would be: A. A. Hodge, *The Confession of Faith*; G. I. Williamson, *The Westminster Confession of Faith*; John Murray, *Redemption Accomplished and Applied*; and W. C. Robinson, *The Reformation: A Rediscovery of Grace*. Questions for thought:

1. What is the difference between the teachings in our confession on justification and those of Roman Catholicism, Dispensationalism, and modern humanism?
2. Why is man completely dependent on Christ alone for his justification?
3. What results does justification have on our understanding of sin?
4. What does Chapter Eleven on justification teach us about "one church, one Lord, one faith, one baptism?"

Chapter Twelve
Of Adoption

CONFESSION OF FAITH

1. All those that are justified, God vouchsafeth, in and for his only Son Jesus Christ, to make partakers of the grace of adoption, by which they are taken into the number, and enjoy the liberties and privileges of the children of God, have his name put upon them, receive the Spirit of adoption, have access to the throne of grace with boldness, are enabled to cry, Abba, Father, are pitied, protected, provided for, and chastened by him, as by a father: yet never cast off, but sealed to the day of redemption; and inherit the promises, as heirs of everlasting salvation.

WHAT A BEAUTIFUL one-paragraph statement is found in Chapter Twelve of the Westminster Confession of Faith and titled "Of Adoption." One cannot read the words of the confession and hail man's genius, though such a temptation does arise. Instead, the wisdom of God has to be spotlighted, especially as one sees how the Holy Spirit gave men such consistent insight on his Word in formulating doctrine.

Every Christian should be able to understand and explain his or her relationship to God. Yet such an obvious knowledge is not always present in one's testimony. Chapter Twelve is precise, and worth committing to memory. This stated truth is a great advance in one's assurance of redemption.

The major theme of the chapter is how the justified person becomes a member of God's family. It elucidates the manifold privileges that belong to the adopted child of God.

Let us first remember that in the general area of creation, God is the Father of us all. There is some general truth to the universal Fatherhood of God; however, though all men have God as their Creator-Father, not all men are special children of God with privileges of sonship.

To become a member of God's chosen family, the Father had to choose, the Son had to die a propitiatory death, and the Holy Spirit has to apply Christ's saving work to the believer's heart. We have no less than the Triune God to praise for our redemption. All three persons of the Godhead played an active part.

What the doctrine of adoption emphasizes is that we are doubly God's, by creation and redemption. God has done what had to be done in order to deal with our sins, to enable us to repent and believe, and to take us into his family.

Christ Jesus has justified us, an act of declaring us not guilty because of his saving work. This act of justification is absolutely essential before one can become a member of God's family.

The whole personal relationship between God and his chosen ones is underscored here. Justification reflects one aspect of God's love, namely his forgiveness, and it also reflects and sets in motion the whole process of God's love in bringing us into his family.

The opening statement uses the phrase "grace of adoption." This underscores that our whole redemption is by God's grace through faith.

When believers are taken into the family of God, the new relationship brings certain privileges and responsibilities. The first privilege mentioned here is that believers are taken into the number of God's children. We are not redeemed in isolation, but are among others.

As God's children, we are no longer slaves to sin nor do we have to sin. God has freed us from sin's power. He has made us eternally alive to his reality. He has made us new creatures in Christ. He has given us forgiveness, purpose, and meaning.

He has also shared his name with us. We are called Christians. We bear the name of Jesus Christ. We also have free access to God's throne. Where the door to God's throne room was once shut, it is now open to God's children. To come before God, we do not have to go through a human mediator, but only through Christ. How amazing that anyone could have access to the holy God, yet all repentant sinners do. Jesus said, "Whoever comes to me I will never drive away" (John 6:37). We can commune with God, not as our enemy but as "Abba, Father" (Rom. 8:15). There is so much significance in those words. Our deity is not the God of darkness but the Father of light. He is the Father of life, not death. I guess one could say this is a family doctrine. Notice the terms: Father, Son, children, family. There are no strangers in God's family. He knows us by name, even the number of hairs on our heads.

God's children "are pitied, protected, provided for, and chastened by him as by a father." God never leaves us alone to receive only what we deserve, but sees to it that we receive all that he wills for us to have. He also administers whatever discipline we need in order to promote holiness of life. Hebrews 12:6 reminds us that chastening or fatherly discipline is one of the evidences of sonship. In this same line, David could say to God, "It was good for me to be afflicted so that I might learn your decrees" (Ps. 119:71).

The last privilege mentioned is that we are never cast off, but sealed; i.e., we shall inherit his promises, especially everlasting life.

Once God's seal is placed on us and our names are recorded in the Lamb's Book of Life, we shall never perish. We are his forever. We cannot be a child of God today but not tomorrow. God's adoption is certain to all who are called, converted, and justified. He always finishes what he starts. As Christians we are "those who will inherit salvation" (Heb. 1:12, "heirs . . . of the gracious gift of life" (1 Peter 3:7), those who will "inherit the kingdom" (James 2:5), and "heirs of God and co-heirs with Christ" (Rom. 8:17).

Chapter Thirteen
OF SANCTIFICATION

CONFESSION OF FAITH

1. They, who are once effectually called, and regenerated, having a new heart, and a new spirit created in them, are further sanctified, really and personally, through the virtue of Christ's death and resurrection, by his Word and Spirit dwelling in them: the dominion of the whole body of sin is destroyed, and the several lusts thereof are more and more weakened and mortified; and they more and more quickened and strengthened in all saving graces, to the practice of true holiness, without which no man shall see the Lord.

2. This sanctification is throughout, in the whole man; yet imperfect in this life, there abiding still some remnants of corruption in every part; whence ariseth a continual and irreconcilable war, the flesh lusting against the Spirit, and the Spirit against the flesh.

3. In which war, although the remaining corruption, for a time, may much prevail; yet, through the continual supply of strength from the sanctifying Spirit of Christ, the regenerate part doth overcome; and so, the saints grow in grace, perfecting holiness in the fear of God.

SANCTIFICATION is the work of God's grace that begins with one's conversion to Christ Jesus. What was begun in the life of sinners in the new birth, making them new creatures, is continued in sanctification. It is a gradual process, which brings the Christian to a holier life.

This chapter in the Westminster Confession of Faith helps one avoid several misconceptions. One is the idea that salvation is completely from God with man having no responsibility, and another is the equally dangerous thought that man alone is responsible for his salvation. Also avoidable is the error that people can completely overcome sin in this life. These are errors that have popped up throughout church history and particularly in the past 150 years.

It would be helpful to any reader to read this chapter of the confession with the corresponding sections of the Larger and Shorter Catechisms. It is important in the whole chain of salvation, especially in light of the closing words of paragraph one, ". . . to the practice of true holiness, without which no man shall see the Lord." This phrase is taken from Hebrews 12:14, and deals with an area of a person's life that is essential in seeing the Lord.

The first paragraph makes us aware that the sanctification of God's children is real and personal. It is something that happens in the believer himself because ". . . it is God who works in you to will and to act according to his good purpose" (Phil. 2:13).

Four descriptive phrases are used in paragraph one. The **first** is that "the whole body of sin is destroyed." By God's grace the believer is no longer a slave to sin. His enslavement to sin has been transferred to servitude to Jesus. Sin no longer has dominion in the believer's life. It is no longer necessary for a believer to sin. The dominion of sin is broken. We now have a new Master.

The **second** phrase, "the several lusts thereof are more and more weakened and mortified," reminds us that unlike justification, which is an act of a particular moment, sanctification is a continual process. In that process, which continues until we are in heaven, the believer experiences a day by day dying to his lusts. We are not made perfect in life this side of heaven. We do not experience complete victory over sin in this life; however, we do grow in grace, which means we serve sin less and God more. The sinful nature is mortified, i.e., the lusts are more and more put to death.

A **third** phrase in paragraph one refers to our being strengthened in the saving grace. God gives his children strength to sin less and live to righteousness more and more. Where we once could not help but sin, we now have the strength not to sin. The longer we live, the stronger we ought to find ourselves. Where we once desired sin, we now desire sin less and less. God's grace has given us strength to say no to our lusts.

The **fourth** part of the paragraph drives home the truth that no man can see the Lord without holiness of life. We must live like Christians. We must practice godliness of life. The confession, following 2 Corinthians 7:1 and Hebrews 12:14, makes it clear that only the pure in heart will see God. As the Beatitudes say, "Blessed are the pure in heart, for they will see God"

(Matt. 5:8). Holiness of life refers both to the principle of holiness and the practice or demonstration of it.

If sanctification is real and personal, it affects the way we live, think, and feel. It enables us once more to be a visible representation of the invisible God, whose image we bear.

Paragraph two is helpful in further defining sanctification. It teaches us that sanctification influences the totality of our lives. God leaves no area of one's life untouched by his sanctifying work. The mind, heart, will, and body are all renewed in holiness. However, the confession is quite clear in several things: one, sanctification has not yet been completed in any Christian this side of heaven. It is the goal toward which every Christian is directed, but it is not completed here and now, nor will it ever be during a person's lifetime. The emphasis of the "victorious life," the "higher life," and the "perfectionist" movements, which teach that one can achieve complete victory over sin in this life, is contrary to the Westminster Standards and their scriptural foundation.

There are remnants of corruption and sin in every person's life. No Christian is exempt from spiritual warfare.

There have been many theories developed in order to bypass the idea that sanctification is a process. Most of those theories have grown out of Greek philosophers' views of man and good and evil, rather than out of scriptural teaching. The truth is that there are no perfect Christians on earth. This is so important to realize. It is also essential to realize that we are not all at the same growth level.

Paragraph three is helpful in dispelling childish attitudes such as: "If I cannot overcome sin, I am not going to fight it!" The confession reminds us that though we struggle with sin and corruption, and at times we think that we are going backward, "through a continual supply of strength from the sanctifying Spirit of Christ, the regenerate part doth overcome . . . ." In him we are more than conquerors. "He who began a good work in you will carry it on to completion until the day of Christ Jesus" (Phil. 1:6). Victory is certain. Our last enemy, death, will be destroyed. God is at work in our lives.

Christians must never embrace a hyper-Calvinistic view of salvation that teaches that God does everything and man does nothing. That is true of regeneration, justification, and glorification, but in the whole picture of redemption we know that man is responsible to believe in Christ and repent of his sins. He is responsible to strive against and flee from sin, and to do good works.

We must never be tempted to believe that all we must do is simply trust in Christ. Though that is the basis of it all, God calls us to a life of personal activity in growth. We cannot adopt the childish attitude that says, "All right, Lord, if you do not want me to commit this or that sin, you must do it, I cannot!"

The beauty of salvation comes in realizing that we can do whatever God tells us to do or not to do because he is at work in our lives. After we are born again and from that moment on, we are co-laborers in Christ.

Chapter Fourteen
OF SAVING FAITH

CONFESSION OF FAITH

1. The grace of faith, whereby the elect are enabled to believe to the saving of their souls, is the work of the Spirit of Christ in their hearts, and is ordinarily wrought by the ministry of the Word, by which also, and by the administration of the sacraments, and prayer, it is increased and strengthened.

2. By this faith, a Christian believeth to be true whatsoever is revealed in the Word, for the authority of God himself speaking therein; and acteth differently upon that which each particular passage thereof containeth; yielding obedience to the commands, trembling at the threatenings, and embracing the promises of God for this life, and that which is to come. But the principal acts of saving faith are accepting, receiving, and resting upon Christ alone for justification, sanctification, and eternal life, by virtue of the covenant of grace.

3. This faith is different in degrees, weak or strong; may be often and many ways assailed, and weakened, but gets the victory: growing up in many to the attainment of a full assurance, through Christ, who is both the author and finisher of our faith.

THE WESTMINSTER Confession of Faith speaks of twin graces: saving faith and repentance unto life. Actually, they are heads and tails of the same coin. They do not exist apart from each other. Though each formulates itself into its own doctrine, they are equally necessary for salvation.

It would be academic to argue whether one precedes the other in the application of redemption. The Westminster Confession takes up saving faith first; therefore, we shall begin there.

If one looks at a harmony of the Westminster Standards, one sees that they speak of saving faith in a broad sense. The Larger Catechism speaks of justifying faith. The Shorter Catechism speaks of faith.

One may wonder why this chapter does not follow the chapter on effectual calling. We would think that the Westminster divines would have followed this structure of life in the Shorter and Larger Catechisms. They had merely spoken of justifying faith on faith alone. The WCF definition is broader and more inclusive than a simple reference to the initial act of faith; so it is there, but the fuller use of saving faith is there also. This definition could actually be located anywhere within the doctrine of salvation.

The WCF appears to be emphasizing not only what we see as the beginning evidence of the new birth, namely faith and repentance, but also of the ongoing faith within the believer. Some systematic theologians do the same thing, speaking of faith specifically in the area of justifying faith but then generally in the whole of the Christian life.

Let us proceed to see how Chapter Fourteen defines saving faith. It might be helpful to study the sequence of saving faith in a Christian's life. We would begin with paragraph two: "The principal acts of saving faith are accepting, receiving, and resting upon Christ alone for justification, sanctification, and eternal life, by virtue of the covenant of grace."

Once a person is born again by the power of God, that new life automatically leads him to conversion. Conversion involves saving faith and repentance. The new mind and heart bring with them knowledge of the truth of Christ, a commitment to him and a trust or belief in his power to save. The WCF states that the Christian accepts, receives, and rests in Christ alone for justification. He cannot save himself. Others cannot save him. Jesus alone is the Savior; therefore, he learns that Christ is the only Redeemer. He trusts him alone for eternal life.

Not only does the saving faith apply to justification, it also applies to sanctification and eternal life. All areas of salvation grow out of saving faith within the covenant of grace context (paragraph two).

The definition given in paragraph two continues to be a helpful summary in presenting the gospel to non-Christians. It helps clarify to an individual just what saving faith involves: "accepting, receiving, and resting upon Christ alone for justification, sanctification, and eternal life, by virtue of the covenant of grace."

How can one accept, receive, and rest in Christ alone for salvation? Paragraph one explains it simply: by the Holy Spirit's gracious work in sinners' hearts. Though saving faith involves the deliberate act of a sinner made new by God's power, the faith is received by the Holy Spirit. "For it is by grace you have been saved, through faith—and this not from yourselves, it is the gift of God—not by works, so that no one can boast" (Eph. 2:8–9).

How does the Holy Spirit bring faith to one's heart? Ordinarily, it is by the Word of God. As Paul says to the Roman Christians, "Faith comes from hearing the message, and the message is heard through the word of Christ" (Rom. 10:17). Along with the Word of God, we are given prayer and the sacraments of baptism and the Lord's Supper as means of increasing and strengthening that faith. Saving faith may begin as small as a grain of mustard seed, but it is cultivated and strengthened by the ministry of the Word, sacraments, and prayer. All these are indispensable to a believer's growth in grace.

This chapter explains and reminds us that God deals with us as individuals, and we may be at different stages even in the matter of faith. Though all true saving faith will involve the above-stated elements, it may differ among individuals. Mr. A's faith may not be as strong as Mr. B's. But as long as it is true saving faith, this is all that God requires.

Paragraph three explains that this saving faith is not static. Certain circumstances may weaken and/or strengthen our faith. However, regardless of whether a situation causes our faith to be weakened or strengthened, if it is saving faith, it will bring victory.

This is another testimony to the sovereign grace of God. One cannot lose his saving faith. Though the reality of the Lord and the Christian life may be dimmed at times, and though some may feel cut off, the result of saving faith is victory. This will be dealt with more fully under the chapters about perseverance of the saints and assurance of salvation.

In Luke 22:32, we read, "But I have prayed for you, Simon, that your faith may not fail. And when you have turned back, strengthen your brothers." Jesus prays for his own. He keeps his own. None of the elect shall perish, because Christ is the author and finisher of our faith.

Let us also remember saving faith in the general sense. Paragraph two underscores that saving faith accepts whatever God reveals in his Word as truth. God said it in the Word. I believe it. In addition, we obey God's commands by faith. We tremble at his warning and embrace the promises of God for this life and the life to come.

Use this chapter in determining what is true saving faith. Be certain in your life and witness that you have a clear understanding of it. Understand that it is a gift of God's grace that enables man to receive the gospel of Christ. Faith is God-generated, and it is developed by God as we follow his Word obediently.

All men have faith, but not all men have saving faith. Those whom God has chosen, those for whom he sent His Son to die on Calvary, and those born again from above are the ones who possess saving faith.

Questions to consider: Who has saving faith? Does each person have the same amount of saving faith? Can one lose saving faith? What are the elements of saving faith? What is its end result?

Chapter Fifteen
OF REPENTANCE UNTO LIFE

CONFESSION OF FAITH

1. Repentance unto life is an evangelical grace, the doctrine whereof is to be preached by every minister of the gospel, as well as that of faith in Christ.

2. By it, a sinner, out of the sight and sense not only of the danger, but also of the filthiness and odiousness of his sins, as contrary to the holy nature, and righteous law of God; and upon the apprehension of his mercy in Christ to such as are penitent, so grieves for, and hates his sins, as to turn from them all unto God, purposing and endeavoring to walk with him in all the ways of his commandments.

3. Although repentance be not to be rested in, as any satisfaction for sin, or any cause of the pardon thereof, which is the act of God's free grace in Christ; yet it is of such necessity to all sinners, that none may expect pardon without it.

4. As there is no sin so small, but it deserves damnation; so there is no sin so great, that it can bring damnation upon those who truly repent.

5. Men ought not to content themselves with a general repentance, but it is every man's duty to endeavor to repent of his particular sins, particularly.

6. As every man is bound to make private confession of his sins to God, praying for the pardon thereof; upon which, and the forsaking of them, he shall find mercy; so, he that scandalizeth his brother, or the church of Christ, ought to be willing, by a private or public confession, and sorrow for his sin, to declare his repentance to those that are offended, who are thereupon to be reconciled to him, and in love to receive him.

IN THE LAST CHAPTER, we looked at the Westminster Confession of Faith's teaching on saving faith. Chapter Fifteen deals with its twin grace of repentance. The way the WCF presents the subjects of saving faith and repentance reminds us that you cannot have one without the other. Some have maintained that preaching saving faith is all that is necessary, and that repentance is so much a part of saving faith that it needs no special emphasis.

The confession certainly disagrees with that approach, and serves to illustrate the closeness of the two doctrines. We must preach, teach, and demonstrate both saving faith and repentance unto life. The WCF contains six paragraphs on this important subject. The first paragraph underscores that because repentance of sin is an evangelical grace, it is to be proclaimed by every minister of the gospel, and of course by those actively involved in personal evangelism.

The normal explanation of conversion is that it contains the two elements of saving faith and repentance of sins. In order for a person to experience God's redemption, he must believe and repent. Both are part of the sinner's obligations in order to be saved.

Having explained saving faith, let us examine closely the WCF's definition of repentance to life. It begins its definition in paragraph two, which contains both the ground of repentance and the proper ingredients.

The ground of our repentance grows out of the truth that we are hell-deserving sinners. As we look at ourselves in light of the holy God and his righteous law, we see in paragraph two our danger and our sins' "filthiness and odiousness . . . as contrary to the holy nature, and righteous law of God. . . ." Recall Isaiah's experience as he saw himself before the holy God. "Woe is me! for I am undone; because I am a man of unclean lips, and I dwell in the midst of a people of unclean lips; for mine eyes have seen the King, Jehovah of hosts" (Isa. 6:5 ASV).

The Larger and Shorter Catechism questions 76 and 87, respectively, contain words almost identical to those of the WCF. All three documents refer to the ground and ingredients of true repentance. They are helpful in reminding us what is and is not repentance of sins. That's important. If repentance is an essential part of one's redemption, it must be truly exercised and demonstrated.

What is involved in true repentance? Paragraph two underscores four necessary parts: **First**, the acknowledgement of sins; **second**, the grief and sorrow of those sins; **third**, the turning away from them and toward the

Lord; and **fourth**, the conscious desire not to sin but rather to walk in the ways of God's commandments. Sorrow for sin is not to be mistaken for repentance. Though it is an aspect of repentance, it is only one of four elements. The Bible says that godly sorrow leads to repentance. Even unbelievers can experience a certain sorrow and regret because of their wrongdoing. Only godly sorrow leads to repentance.

Can a person really be saved without this kind of repentance? If not, does it imply that Christ's atoning death was not enough to merit our forgiveness? Paragraph three addresses that point. Our only hope of salvation is in Christ alone. We can only rest in him, not the labors of our hands. His death is the only hope that we have for pardon. However, although salvation is of God's free grace, he has established the application of his redemption in such a manner that no one can ever expect to be pardoned, forgiven, and received without genuine repentance. God who determines the beginning and end of salvation also determines the means. One cannot hope to be saved without true repentance.

But are some sins more serious than others? If so, are they not really the ones for which we need to repent? Some Christians have tried to live on that premise; however, paragraph four states that all sins, large and small, equally bring damnation on sinners. The opposite is also true. When one truly repents, God forgives all sins large and small. One must be careful both in preaching and personal evangelism to avoid the impression that one need only repent of big sins. One must also be careful in dealing with wounded, grief-stricken sinners to clearly show that upon true repentance, God forgives the sinner and removes the sins from the sinner's account.

Growing out of this, paragraph five urges all sinners to give careful examination in attending to the need for repentance. Do not just do so generally—"Lord forgive all my sins"—but rather, "Lord forgive this sin of omission and this sin of commission." Repent of all particular sins. This calls for self-examination not only before the Lord's Supper but constantly, even daily. Remember too, if it is genuine repentance, it is coupled with saving faith. Therefore it is not a constant morbid crucifying of self for sins committed. It is taking God at his word and receiving his forgiveness.

The WCF closes this chapter with one other area of biblical truth. Confession of sin is a matter of the heart. Every sinner should make his private confession to the Lord; however, some sins are not just private in nature. We do not sin in a vacuum. This means that there is a **fifth** element that adds to true repentance in certain cases. When a Christian's sin offends or hurts a brother, repentance must be demonstrated to that brother. If the sin is of such public knowledge that it scandalizes or gives the church a black eye, then public repentance is to be made.

Those of us who have the responsibility and privilege of counseling with guilt-ridden people need to be very careful not to neglect all five elements of repentance. Public repentance and going to an offended brother are part of God's prescription for true forgiveness. We must not encourage a person to stop short of the full requirements. Nor should we fail to emphasize to the offended brother or group the forgiving attitude that they should express to the penitent sinner.

This chapter reminds us that sin is a serious matter to God. We cannot afford to neglect this area of repentance for this life and the life to come. Much healing can and will take place in relationships if sin is properly disposed of; otherwise, estrangement will remain and hostility and resentment will be the painful results.

Chapter Sixteen
Of Good Works

Confession of Faith

1. Good works are only such as God hath commanded in his holy Word, and not such as, without the warrant thereof, are devised by men, out of blind zeal, or upon any pretense of good intention.

2. These good works, done in obedience to God's commandments, are the fruits and evidences of a true and lively faith: and by them believers manifest their thankfulness, strengthen their assurance, edify their brethren, adorn the profession of the gospel, stop the mouths of the adversaries, and glorify God, whose workmanship they are, created in Christ Jesus thereunto, that, having their fruit unto holiness, they may have the end, eternal life.

3. Their ability to do good works is not at all of themselves, but wholly from the Spirit of Christ. And that they may be enabled thereunto, beside the graces they have already received, there is required an actual influence of the same Holy Spirit, to work in them to will, and to do, of his good pleasure: yet are they not hereupon to grow negligent, as if they were not bound to perform any duty unless upon a special motion of the Spirit; but they ought to be diligent in stirring up the grace of God that is in them.

4. They who, in their obedience, attain to the greatest height which is possible in this life, are so far from being able to supererogate, and to do more than God requires, as that they fall short of much which in duty they are bound to do.

5. We cannot by our best works merit pardon of sin, or eternal life at the hand of God, by reason of the great disproportion that is between them and the glory to come; and the infinite distance that is between us and God, whom, by them, we can neither profit, nor satisfy for the debt of our former sins, but when we have done all we can, we have done but our duty, and are unprofitable servants: and because, as they are good, they proceed from his Spirit; and as they are wrought by us, they are defiled, and mixed with so

much weakness and imperfection, that they cannot endure the severity of God's judgment.

6.   Notwithstanding, the persons of believers being accepted through Christ, their good works also are accepted in him; not as though they were in this life wholly unblamable and unreprovable in God's sight; but that he, looking upon them in his Son, is pleased to accept and reward that which is sincere, although accompanied with many weaknesses and imperfections.

7.   Works done by unregenerate men, although for the matter of them they may be things which God commands; and of good use both to themselves and others: yet, because they proceed not from an heart purified by faith; nor are done in a right manner, according to the Word; nor to a right end, the glory of God, they are therefore sinful, and cannot please God, or make a man meet to receive grace from God: and yet, their neglect of them is more sinful and displeasing unto God.

IT IS NOT surprising to find seven sections in the Westminster Confession of Faith on the subject of "good works." This was one of the main points of the Reformation. The church of Rome had developed a belief that one's salvation from sin was impossible without the merits of good works. The church's emphasis was that good works were essential in completing the process of salvation. This made the twin points for Rome's view of salvation to be faith and works.

Just as it was necessary for the WCF to contain a lengthy definition of good works for the mid-seventeenth century, so is it essential for this subject to be restudied today. One would observe that many Roman Catholics vacillate between the two extremes of exalting good works or neglecting them altogether.

The WCF makes it very clear that good works can neither be neglected nor given the wrong priority. You will find the best balance on this subject, faithful to the Scriptures, in capsule form in Chapter Sixteen.

Chapter Sixteen discusses: a definition of good works, the place of good works in God's scheme of salvation, how one is able to perform good works, how good works are not meritorious, and how good works will be taken into account by God in judgment. Paragraph seven is very helpful in relating how unbelievers do outwardly some of the same works that Christians perform and yet do not please God.

Each of the chapter's seven sections deserves a separate study. We would hope that you would take the time to examine them in greater depth. Excellent reading material on the subject includes: Gordon Clark, *What Do Presbyterians Believe?*; G. L. Williamson, *The Westminster Confession of Faith*; A. A. Hodge, *The Confession of Faith*; John Murray, *Redemption Accomplished and Applied*; and Louis Berkhof, *Systematic Theology*.

The **first** section of Chapter Sixteen makes it clear that good works are only those things commanded in God's holy Word. They are not left to the definition of men.

Helping in a community project or showing kindness for humanitarian reasons may or may not be a good work. Only those things commanded by God and done out of a sincere heart response to his Word will qualify. Some things that we do may or may not qualify as good works; therefore, it is dangerous to hang one's hope of salvation on good works.

The **second** section shows where good works fit in the whole plan. We see in the first section that saving faith is the cause of good works. They are fruits of saving faith. If this is true, then we cannot base our justification on good works nor can we earn our salvation. However, this does not validate the claim of some modernists that good works are no longer required.

This second section has given birth to a helpful statement: "We are saved by faith alone but by a faith that is not alone." True saving faith produces good works. There is such a cause-and-effect relationship that it would be proper to evaluate the reality of saving faith according to good works. As James says, "Faith without deeds [works] is dead" (James 2:26b).

Section **three** answers the question of how a person can perform good works. The response is simply that good works can only be performed by a person who is indwelt by the Spirit of Christ. Good works do not precede the new birth and conversion. They follow these acts of God. This does not imply that a professing Christian can sit and refrain from good works until he is dramatically moved by the Holy Spirit. Believers indwelt by God's Spirit must not only be subject to the Spirit's leadership—they must be diligently stirring up the grace of God that is in them.

Sections **four, five,** and **six** bring us back to the historical perspective from which the confession was written to make a clear distinction between the teaching of Protestant Christianity and that of Rome.

The Roman Catholic Church had a doctrine called "Supererogation." Under that doctrine, not only did works have meritorious effect, but a person could do more than required for his salvation and store up a surplus of good works for others. Sections four and five deal with the awful notion that man can do more than God requires of him.

We cannot earn our pardon from sin by good works. Under the original covenant of works established with but broken by Adam, good works were possible, and they kept Adam and Eve in original righteousness. But after the fall of man into sin, things changed drastically. Good works cannot earn our justification and pardon. We can never hope to do enough good works to outweigh our bad works. Pardon from sin cannot come to us in that manner.

Even our best is defiled and mixed with weakness and imperfection. Only the perfect sacrifice of Jesus Christ could pay our debt; however, as section six indicates, as God accepts believers in Christ so does he accept their works done in Christ. But why all the trouble to perform good works if they will not make us acceptable in God's sight? There are a couple reasons: First, good works are genuine evidence and fruit of saving faith, according to paragraph two. Second, God will reward us according to our good works, we read in paragraph six.

While no one dare think his acceptance by God is based on good works, no one dare presume that he possesses saving faith and acceptance with God without good works. We cannot omit the necessity of good works in the Christian life, but we must not allow them to be used in an unbiblical manner that suggests they earn salvation, for us or for others.

The **last** section explains a problem that perplexes people. The confusion comes from not understanding sections one through six; however, it is included to complete the subject of good works.

We have seen that good works can only be performed by those indwelt by God's Spirit. But to put it another way, section seven says that works done by an unbeliever, even though they may outwardly resemble the good works of the Christian life, are not good and cannot please God. Why?

Because they are not done from a regenerate heart with the desire to please God, and are not done in the right manner. The whole motivation is wrong.

God looks at the heart. He considers our motives even more than the outward deed. A corrupt tree cannot produce good fruit, as the New Testament teaches, yet the last sentence of the chapter is priceless: "And yet, their neglect of them [the unbeliever's neglect of good works] is more sinful and displeasing unto God." The Bible teaches that the rewards of believers are determined by their obedience and good works, but the opposite is taught regarding unbelievers. Jesus said that some unbelievers will suffer a greater portion of God's wrath than other unbelievers (cf. Luke 12:47–48).

The summary of Chapter Sixteen is that "it is by grace you have been saved, through faith," and. "we are God's workmanship, created in Christ Jesus to do good works" (Eph. 2:8, 10).

We are saved by faith alone but by a faith that is not alone. "'Blessed are the dead who die in the Lord from now on.' 'Yes,' says the Spirit, 'they will rest from their labor, for their deeds will follow them.'" (Rev. 14:13).

Chapter Seventeen
Of the Perseverance of the Saints

Confession of Faith

1. They, whom God hath accepted in his Beloved, effectually called, and sanctified by his Spirit, can neither totally nor finally fall away from the state of grace, but shall certainly persevere therein to the end, and be eternally saved.

2. This perseverance of the saints depends not upon their own free will, but upon the immutability of the decree of election, flowing from the free and unchangeable love of God the Father; upon the efficacy of the merit and intercession of Jesus Christ, the abiding of the Spirit, and of the seed of God within them, and the nature of the covenant of grace: from all which ariseth also the certainty and infallibility thereof.

3. Nevertheless, they may, through the temptations of Satan and of the world, the prevalency of corruption remaining in them, and the neglect of the means of their preservation, fall into grievous sins; and, for a time, continue therein: whereby they incur God's displeasure, and grieve his Holy Spirit, come to be deprived of some measure of their graces and comforts, have their hearts hardened, and their consciences wounded; hurt and scandalize others, and bring temporal judgments upon themselves.

How long does one's salvation last? Is it a day-to-day proposition only? Or, is it longer? Does it last forever? Or, can it be lost at any given point? People have been asking such questions for centuries. Today is no exception.

Ideas, lifestyles, and cultures change from people to people but the deep-seated questions do not vary much. Chapter Seventeen of the Westminster Confession of Faith deals with one of these significant questions: can a Christian lose his salvation? You will find some who say "yes" with great certainty, but the answer is too important for us to settle for men's conclusions. We must ask God the Savior for the answer.

As with other doctrines, the confession brings together in three brief paragraphs the teachings of the written Word of God on this subject. It says: **First**, once a person has been called and sanctified by God's Spirit, he can never fall away from the state of grace; **second**, true believers will persevere or keep on until the end and be saved; **third**, a believer's perseverance is assured because God works in him; and **fourth**, a believer can backslide from time to time and incur God's displeasure, and lose some of the privileges of a Christian. Let's examine these points more closely:

First, a true believer in Jesus Christ can never fall from the state of grace. Salvation in all of its parts is like the whole, completely dependent on God.

A true Christian cannot become a non-Christian. Once God begins his saving work in our lives, that work cannot fail to be completed, as Paul said so clearly in Philippians 1:6: "He who began a good work in you will carry it on to completion until the day of Christ Jesus." God completes what he starts, and we can have confidence in God's faithfulness and consistency. He gives us his word that "no one can snatch them [his sheep] out of my hand" (John 10:28).

However, if this is all that someone sees ("once saved, always saved"), he sees only the one side of salvation that says man has no responsibility, and that God does it all. This would have us believe that it is God who perseveres. Now God does not change in response to man's action, but man does have a part to play. This is why the doctrine is called "perseverance of the saints" and not perseverance of God.

The **second** point emphasizes this angle. True believers will persevere in the faith. True, we can fall from grace, as both Galatians and Hebrews teach, but we cannot fall out of the state (condition) of grace. We will keep on in the faith. While it is true that God saves us and keeps us, we must be obedient. Each time the Scriptures speak of our salvation being in God's hand, and therefore secure, it is always in the context of our persevering. In John 10 it is those who hear and follow the Lord who are secure in Christ. In Philippians 2 it is God working in us both to will and to do according to his good pleasure, but it is also our working out our own salvation with fear and trembling.

But how do Christians do this? We are still troubled and influenced by sin. The **third** point found in section two gives us a clue. God preserves us. He keeps us. We are held by his all-powerful hand. We can know with great certainty that if God begins his saving work in us, he will not leave the work unfinished. He will watch over us and keep us so that we cannot fall away and lose our salvation. The confession draws our attention to the truth that our perseverance does not rest upon sinful man, but rather on the unchangeable love of God the Father, the sufficiency of Jesus Christ and the abiding Holy Spirit, plus the seed that God has placed within each believer.

God's nature, which is always expressed in his work, is the most important element in the truth of the perseverance of the saints. Our hope is not in our own faithfulness and dependability, but rather in God who never changes.

Does this mean Christians never sin, or that if Christians do sin, it does not really matter? Not in the least. Because we are not yet made perfect (and will not be in this lifetime), we are still besieged by sin. Satan continues to tempt us. We can begin to neglect the means of perseverance and fall into grievous sin—and continue in that rebellious state for a while. This is what we call "backsliding."

Christians can backslide. Abraham, David, and Peter are classic biblical examples. What happens to the backslider? We know that if he is a Christian, he cannot fall from the state of grace. But he can incur God's displeasure as the Lord removes his graces and comfort from that person. The backslider can experience a wounded conscience, and even hurt others.

As we see in the next chapter, the backslider does not lose his salvation. But he can and should lose his assurance of salvation. He should be treated as though he were not a believer because the remedy for the nonbeliever and the backslider is the same: repentance of sin and faith in Jesus Christ. The difference between the two is seen in their responses. The backslider, being a true but disobedient believer, will repent and come back to God as Abraham, David, and Peter did. The non-Christian will not.

Every Christian must be concerned about sin in his life. He cannot allow himself to toy with sin, nor can he afford to keep unconfessed sins in his life.

The Christian must hear God's warning that "he who stands firm to the end will be saved" (Matt. 24:13). God has been pleased to tell us about Abraham, David, and Peter's falling into sin to show us that Christians can fall if they fail to persevere. But if we do backslide, then as true believers we will repent and return to the Lord.

Christians must be stirred to persevere and live an obedient and submissive life. This doctrine challenges and encourages us to follow after God. It assures us that we will, because of God.

Chapter Eighteen

Of the Assurance of Grace and Salvation

Confession of Faith

1. Although hypocrites and other unregenerate men may vainly deceive themselves with false hopes and carnal presumptions of being in the favor of God, and estate of salvation (which hope of theirs shall perish): yet such as truly believe in the Lord Jesus, and love him in sincerity, endeavoring to walk in all good conscience before him, may, in this life, be certainly assured that they are in the state of grace, and may rejoice in the hope of the glory of God, which hope shall never make them ashamed.

2. This certainty is not a bare conjectural and probable persuasion grounded upon a fallible hope; but an infallible assurance of faith founded upon the divine truth of the promises of salvation, the inward evidence of those graces unto which these promises are made, the testimony of the Spirit of adoption witnessing with our spirits that we are the children of God, which Spirit is the earnest of our inheritance, whereby we are sealed to the day of redemption.

3. This infallible assurance doth not so belong to the essence of faith, but that a true believer may wait long, and conflict with many difficulties before he be partaker of it: yet, being enabled by the Spirit to know the things which are freely given him of God, he may, without extraordinary revelation, in the right use of ordinary means, attain thereunto. And therefore it is the duty of everyone to give all diligence to make his calling and election sure, that thereby his heart may be enlarged in peace and joy in the Holy Ghost, in love and thankfulness to God, and in strength and cheerfulness in the duties of obedience, the proper fruits of this assurance; so far is it from inclining men to looseness.

4. True believers may have the assurance of their salvation divers ways shaken, diminished, and intermitted; as, by negligence in preserving of it, by falling into some special sin which woundeth the conscience and grieveth the Spirit; by some sudden or vehement temptation, by God's withdrawing the light of

his countenance, and suffering even such as fear him to walk in darkness and to have no light: yet are they never utterly destitute of that seed of God, and life of faith, that love of Christ and the brethren, that sincerity of heart, and conscience of duty, out of which, by the operation of the Spirit, this assurance may, in due time, be revived; and by the which, in the meantime, they are supported from utter despair.

THOUGH IT HAS been said that we are not living in a creed-making age, we must disagree with such a statement, with certain qualifications. It is true that the church is not generating healthy creeds today; nevertheless, creeds are being made. One creed of modern Christianity relates to assurance of grace and salvation.

We could call that creed or doctrine "easy believism." One needs only to read a book such as *What's Gone Wrong with the Harvest* by H. Wilbert Norton and James F. Engel or *Contemporary Christian Communication, Its Theory and Practice* by James F. Engel to see that a lot of the claims about people making "decisions for Christ" are only claims, because the fruit of true discipleship is missing.

Jesus said in Matthew 7:22–23, "Many will say to me on that day, 'Lord, Lord, did we not prophesy in your name . . . ?' Then I will tell them plainly, 'I never knew you.'" There are two false impressions created by the modern creed of "easy believism" that are dangerous. **First**, one can understand it to imply that he can be a Christian if he has "faith" in Jesus Christ, regardless of his lifestyle. A **second** dangerous teaching is that if one does not have assurance of his salvation, then he must not be saved. This is based on the false assumption that assurance is an essential ingredient to being saved.

Chapter Eighteen masterfully draws us back to the biblical testimony that suppresses delusion, false hope, or hopelessness. Let us briefly analyze this chapter.

First, the chapter says there are people who believe they are saved—they have been baptized, catechized, and enrolled as communing members of the church—but they are hypocrites. They have deceived themselves and others by presuming to be Christians. The confession goes on to state, on the other hand, that a true believer who loves the Lord and lives a good

83

Christian life may certainly possess the assurance of being in the state of grace. He will not deny the Lord, nor be ashamed to profess the Christian faith.

Second, the confession carefully defines the basis of one's hope of assurance and of being in the state of grace. One can be outwardly convinced of his spirituality, only to be deluded; however, infallible assurance grows out of the truth of God's promise. A true believer will experience and demonstrate the working of God in his life. He will love the Lord in word and deed. His faith will generate fruit:

There will also be an inward working of the Holy Spirit that bears witness with the believer that he is a child of God. Hence, he will not fear that the Lord will say to him, "I never knew you." He will be "sealed for the day of redemption" (Eph. 4:30). He will know that God has begun a good work in him and will complete it.

You can see the importance of the confession's wording. In order to have true hope, one must have both the profession of faith in Christ and perseverance.

Third, paragraph three states that assurance of salvation is not essential for one's salvation. It is not biblical to require every Christian to know that he is saved. For some true Christians it takes a long time to experience the peace and assurance that they are God's children. Also, not everyone needs an extraordinary event such as a shipwreck or a bolt of lightning to generate true assurance.

Let us keep several things in mind here. There is a distinction between being saved arid being assured of one's salvation. Do not judge the reality of salvation in a person's life by his assurance.

It is the duty of every Christian to make his calling and election sure, as Peter has instructed (2 Peter 1:3–11). This means that if I am a Christian, rather than living any way I please or living after the world's lawless fashion, I will love the law of God and follow it with all my might.

As Chapter Nineteen will teach, a Christian will not be an antinomian. That is, he will not be opposed to the law of God (defined by the confession), lawless, loose, etc. He will obey the commands of the Lord, and he will structure his life according to God's holy law. This becomes a key to one's assurance of salvation, not that law keeping is the root of a person's salvation but rather the fruit of it. Genuine Christians are hearers and doers of God's Word.

Fourth, the last section of Chapter Eighteen states that a believer can lose his assurance of salvation without losing salvation. However, there are times when a believer's faith may be so shaken, diminished, and intermittent (as by regularly neglecting to do what God says or by committing some specific sin) that his assurance may be lost.

God may allow a person to walk in darkness, a state that St. John of the Cross described as "the dark night of the soul," yet never be utterly destitute of hope. This is where Christians must be careful in their witness and counsel. Do not make assurance of salvation a ground of salvation, but explain that assurance of salvation is attainable by obedience to God. Also, be cautious in giving counsel to those living in unconfessed sin.

While Scripture teaches that nothing can separate Christians from the love of God, the experience of that truth may be brighter or darker at any given time for a believer. Let us not attempt to have a metal mold into which we try to force everyone, as we witness for the Lord. Let us meet people where they are.

Knowledge, understanding, and action upon the content of Chapter Eighteen are vital for our day. Rehearse it, study it, learn it, as you work to make your calling and election sure.

Chapter Nineteen
OF THE LAW OF GOD

CONFESSION OF FAITH

1. God gave to Adam a law, as a covenant of works, by which he bound him and all his posterity to personal, entire, exact, and perpetual obedience, promised life upon the fulfilling, and threatened death upon the breach of it, and endued him with power and ability to keep it.

2. This law, after his fall, continued to be a perfect rule of righteousness; and, as such, was delivered by God upon Mount Sinai, in ten commandments, and written in two tables: the first four commandments containing our duty towards God; and the other six, our duty to man.

3. Beside this law, commonly called moral, God was pleased to give to the people of Israel, as a church under age, ceremonial laws, containing several typical ordinances, partly of worship, prefiguring Christ, his graces, actions, sufferings, and benefits; and partly, holding forth divers instructions of moral duties. All which ceremonial laws are now abrogated, under the new testament.

4. To them also, as a body politic, he gave sundry judicial laws, which expired together with the State of that people; not obliging any other now, further than the general equity thereof may require.

5. The moral law doth forever bind all, as well justified persons as others, to the obedience thereof; and that, not only in regard of the matter contained in it, but also in respect of the authority of God the Creator, who gave it. Neither doth Christ, in the gospel, any way dissolve, but much strengthen this obligation.

6. Although true believers be not under the law, as a covenant of works, to be thereby justified, or condemned; yet is it of great use to them, as well as to others; in that, as a rule of life informing them of the will of God, and their duty, it directs and binds them to walk accordingly; discovering also the

sinful pollutions of their nature, hearts, and lives; so as, examining themselves thereby, they may come to further conviction of, humiliation for, and hatred against sin, together with a clearer sight of the need they have of Christ, and the perfection of his obedience. It is likewise of use to the regenerate, to restrain their corruptions, in that it forbids sin: and the threatenings of it serve to show what even their sins deserve; and what afflictions, in this life, they may expect for them, although freed from the curse thereof threatened in the law. The promises of it, in like manner, show them God's approbation of obedience, and what blessings they may expect upon the performance thereof: although not as due to them by the law as a covenant of works. So as, a man's doing good, and refraining from evil, because the law encourageth to the one, and deterreth from the other, is no evidence of his being under the law; and, not under grace.

7.   Neither are the forementioned uses of the law contrary to the grace of the gospel, but do sweetly comply with it; the Spirit of Christ subduing and enabling the will of man to do that freely, and cheerfully, which the will of God, revealed in the law, requireth to be done.

EACH CHAPTER in the Westminster Confession of Faith displays a uniquely divine providence in the subjects with which it deals. Though the confession is a historical document of the seventeenth century, its topics are those that continue to confront the church.

The subject of the law of God is vital not only to the church but to the world in general simply because all just and right law is a reflection of God's law. Without God's law as our ordering principle, we are left with no absolutes; hence, all is relative to the moment.

This chapter gives a confessional statement regarding God's law. It not only depicts the folly of antinomianism—seen today in the dispensational school of theology, which maintains that the law of God is not for the church because in their system law and grace are incompatible foes—but it also deals with the opposite problem of legalism, which implies that the law is a means of one's justification before God.

The first two paragraphs rehearse the position of the law as a covenant of works, which God gave to Adam. Prior to Adam's fall, he possessed the ability to desire to obey God's law. He was not forced to disobey. Even though Adam chose to disobey God and was changed from a creature of righteousness to one of unrighteousness, the law did not change.

The law was spelled out in detail at Mount Sinai, in the Ten Commandments. In those ten laws, God revealed our continuing duty toward him and toward man. As the law was written on man's heart in the beginning, it was revealed on the tablets of stone at Sinai. It was then summarized both in the five books of Moses and the gospels like this: love God with all your heart, soul, mind, and strength, and your neighbor as yourself.

One would find particular benefit not only from this chapter but also from reading Shorter Catechism questions 39–41 and Larger Catechism questions 91–149. In these documents we are led to understand that the Bible speaks of the law of God in three ways. **First**, there is the moral law; **second**, there is the ceremonial law; and **third**, there is the civil law. It is true in one sense that the law of God is one law, but there is also diversity in God's law in revelation—just as God is both one person and three persons.

Paragraph five explains that the moral law is always binding on both the righteous and unrighteous. Christ does not abrogate the law by the gospel, but rather by the gospel enables the believer to love and obey his law.

Paragraph three states that "ceremonial laws are now abrogated, under the new testament." Why? Because Christ, the one prefigured in the ceremonial law, has come as the once-for-all sacrifice. His coming has superseded and forever done away with the ceremonial law, as A. A. Hodge has stated it.

As far as the civil or judicial law is concerned, paragraph four states, "To them [the Old Testament people of Israel] also, as a body politic, he gave sundry judicial laws, which expired together with the state of that people; not obliging any other now, further than the general equity thereof may require." Paragraphs three, four, and five teach that the ceremonial law is abrogated under the New Testament; the civil law is expired, not obliging any other now; but the moral law is forever binding upon all.

The wisdom of the Westminster divines is shown in this chapter. A balanced perspective of God's law, which is presented here, keeps one from saying that the law of God is not for the church or that the church is bound to those aspects of the law that have been abrogated and have expired with the revelation of the New Testament.

Paragraph four, which states that although the civil law expired with the Old Testament body politic, the general equity undergirding the civil law is still valid; hence, we can maintain that all true and valid law will stem from God who reveals himself in the law. The Larger Catechism's questions 91-149 are particularly helpful in understanding this handling of God's law.

Paragraph seven reminds us that the law properly understood and applied is not contrary to grace, as some maintain; but rather that the law and the gospel are inseparably joined in God's plan of redemption and restoration. Just as it is contrary to Scripture to teach that man is saved by his obedience to the law, so it is wrong for one to believe that the Christian has no further obligation to obey God's law.

There is a modern tendency to set grace and law at irrevocable odds. There are some who would set law and love in deadly combat with each other. The confession, following the biblical language, keeps together law and love, grace and law. It states that moral laws of God provide the principles for men's bodies politic.

The conclusion is that God's law properly understood and applied is indispensable. Without God's law there is chaos. With saving faith in Jesus Christ, the believer is able to live by the law of God as a rule of life. Jesus said, "If you love me, you will obey what I command" (John 14:15).

Chapter Twenty

OF CHRISTIAN LIBERTY, AND THE LIBERTY OF CONSCIENCE

CONFESSION OF FAITH

1. The liberty which Christ hath purchased for believers under the gospel consists in their freedom from the guilt of sin, the condemning wrath of God, the curse of the moral law; and, in their being delivered from this present evil world, bondage to Satan, and dominion of sin; from the evil of afflictions, the sting of death, the victory of the grave, and everlasting damnation; as also, in their free access to God, and their yielding obedience unto him, not out of slavish fear, but a childlike love and willing mind. All which were common also to believers under the law. But, under the new testament, the liberty of Christians is further enlarged, in their freedom from the yoke of the ceremonial law, to which the Jewish church was subjected; and in greater boldness of access to the throne of grace, and in fuller communications of the free Spirit of God, than believers under the law did ordinarily partake of.

2. God alone is Lord of the conscience, and hath left it free from the doctrines and commandments of men, which are, in anything, contrary to his Word; or beside it, if matters of faith, or worship. So that, to believe such doctrines, or to obey such commands, out of conscience, is to betray true liberty of conscience: and the requiring of an implicit faith, and an absolute and blind obedience, is to destroy liberty of conscience, and reason also.

3. They who, upon pretense of Christian liberty, do practice any sin, or cherish any lust, do thereby destroy the end of Christian liberty, which is, that being delivered out of the hands of our enemies, we might serve the Lord without fear, in holiness and righteousness before him, all the days of our life.

4. And because the powers which God hath ordained, and the liberty which Christ hath purchased, are not intended by God to destroy, but mutually to uphold and preserve one another, they who, upon pretense of Christian liberty, shall oppose any lawful power, or the lawful exercise of it, whether it be civil or ecclesiastical, resist the ordinance of God. And, for their publishing of such opinions, or maintaining of such practices, as are contrary to the light

of nature, or to the known principles of Christianity (whether concerning faith, worship, or conversation), or to the power of godliness; or, such erroneous opinions or practices, as either in their own nature, or in the manner of publishing or maintaining them, are destructive to the external peace and order which Christ hath established in the church, they may lawfully be called to account, and proceeded against, by the censures of the church.

THERE IS A TENDENCY to define freedom as the right to do whatever one chooses. This develops into a hedonism that teaches that man is free to do whatever brings him the greatest pleasure.

If we follow through with this idea, we come to Ayn Rand's philosophy of the virtue of selfishness. In emphasizing the idea of individual freedom, her philosophy underscores that what counts the most is one's individual freedom or choice.

In the realm of religion there is an idea abroad today called "liberation theology." This idea is that freedom in Christ implies social, economic, and political freedom as well as religious freedom.

Often "freedom" is tossed around so carelessly that one forgets that before freedom can be discussed and properly observed, the idea of one's master has to be acknowledged. There are many masters among men, and a man is free only to serve his master, whatever or whomever that master may be.

In the Christian context, we must begin by acknowledging that the Lord God of the Bible is our Master. This being true, freedom means freedom to serve him; therefore, we begin with the assumption that freedom has to be defined in light of obedience to our Master. Chapter Twenty of the Westminster Confession of Faith is helpful in underscoring this biblical concept of freedom.

A correct understanding and application of this chapter also helps us to discover a proper definition of Christian liberty. Some have argued that Christian liberty means the right and freedom to do whatever one pleases, because Christians are no longer obligated to obey the law of God.

Notice the arrangement of this subject of Christian liberty within the confession. It follows the chapter on the law of God and precedes the chapter dealing with worship. It contains four sections. Section **one** tells us what Christian liberty is and where it comes from. Section **two** spells out Christian liberty in its broadest sense. Section **three** underscores that Christian liberty is not a license to sin. Section **four** explains the Christian's relationship to church and civil censures. Let us look at each section briefly.

First, what is Christian liberty and where do we find it? Christian liberty is a reference to spiritual freedom. It includes deliverance from the guilt of sin, the condemning wrath of God, and the curse of the moral law. It also has reference to deliverance from the evil world, bondage to Satan, and the dominion of sin, but it also reminds us that the believer has free access to God.

In Old Testament times, the believer was bound to perform certain ceremonial laws. However, in the New Testament, because of the person and work of Christ, the Christian is free from the ceremonial law's demand. Hence, believers today enjoy a greater boldness before the throne of God and a fuller communication of the free Spirit of God.

This liberty is brought to us by Jesus Christ, who purchased our freedom. John said, "So if the Son sets you free, you will be free indeed" (John 8:36). One of the biblical terms used to refer to Jesus Christ is that of Deliverer. Jesus Christ delivered us from all the above by his death, by which he purchased for us the liberty to come before him and the throne of grace.

The freedom and liberty that we have in Christ are a spiritual freedom, which means that regardless of one's political, economic, or social status, Christian liberty can be present in one's heart because "the Lord is the Spirit, and where the Spirit of the Lord is, there is freedom" (2 Cor. 3:17).

Second, what is Christian liberty in connection with one's conscience? Christians are not bound to any master but the Lord God. This means two things. It means first that our conscience is not bound by the teachings of men, particularly when men teach something contrary to God. There is only one Lord of the conscience. Man is not bound before him either by a Pharisaic emphasis on the necessity of man's obedience to certain laws and teachings of men, or by modern fundamentalism's legalistic tendency.

When someone insists that we are bound by things not specified in the

Word of God, they are violating our Christian liberty. Man cannot demand obedience to things contrary to God's Word, nor can man add to God's Word by requiring more spiritual obedience than is written in Scripture.

Jesus said, "'They worship me in vain; their teachings are but rules taught by men'" (Matt. 15:9). This has been a tendency throughout church history, but it violates a Christian's liberty of conscience.

Churches that require things of its members that are either contrary to or over and beyond the Word of God are in no better situation than the Pharisees Jesus denounced.

The **second** meaning of Christian liberty in connection with one's conscience is that it must not be interpreted as license to do whatever one chooses. Section three of Chapter Twenty elaborates on this. Christians who use their liberty as an occasion to "practice any sin, or cherish any lust, do thereby destroy the end of Christian liberty . . . ."

Though the origin of one's Christian liberty is found in the work of Jesus Christ, the preservation of that liberty is closely linked to one's obedience to God and his law. It is hard for people of a legalistic orientation to understand that Christian liberty is not Christian license. Freedom in Christ properly understood simply means that we now can obey the law of God, and that by faithful obedience to God we maintain our Christian liberty.

The Christian is obligated to obey God and do his will, summarily expressed in the Ten Commandments. Because Jesus Christ is our new Master (having liberated us from the old master, Satan), we are now free to obey his will. We are no longer slaves to sin. As section one underscores, our freedom is not freedom from God and his law, but freedom from sin's bondage.

One of the beauties of our Presbyterian and Reformed heritage shines through in this balanced view of Christian liberty. The Reformed faith properly understood and applied will encourage Christian liberty in the same sense as did the Jerusalem council in Acts 15. It will also remind us that Christian liberty is not a license to sin.

Section four completes the subject by explaining the Christian's relationship to church censures. Christians are members of the church of the Lord Jesus Christ and citizens of a certain commonwealth. Power has been given to both the church and the civil authorities to uphold and enforce the law of God. Because the Christian is not yet perfect, he needs policing from both areas in order to preserve his Christian liberty. Freedom necessitates obedience and discipline. God has ordained powers to superintend the believers. Romans13:1 says, "Everyone must submit himself to the governing authorities, for there is no authority except that which God has established." No state government or church judicatory can bind a person's conscience by demanding things contrary to or over and above God's law, but they can and must insist that God's law be obeyed.

Christians cannot oppose the law of God and maintain their Christian liberty at the same time. Believers cannot retain their liberty by themselves. Not only is God's help needed, but so is the assistance of others needed. As long as church leaders and civil authorities rule in accordance with God's Word, Christians must honor their leadership even if it brings censure or discipline to them.

A Christian's conscience is not bound by ecclesiastical or civil pronouncements that are contrary to the law of God. His conscience is only bound by the Word of God. However, careful respect should be demonstrated by Christians toward their leaders because they are ordained by God. Christians should obey the laws of the state unless they are contrary to God's law. Christians should respect the rulings, decisions, and actions of church leaders on the same basis.

Christian liberty is spiritual freedom from sin's bondage. It was purchased for us by Jesus Christ and preserved by our allegiance to him. It is a privilege that calls for working together within God's kingdom in order to keep it. It is not a license to sin, but a freedom to serve.

Christian liberty is not something to be feared by Christians. It does not necessitate the developing of manmade rules and regulations in order to preserve it, as some have done. Christian liberty is the privilege of living in the light of the Word of God and experiencing freedom because slavery to sin has passed away. Because of this, Christians can serve the Lord without fear, in holiness and righteousness before him, all the days of our lives.

Chapter Twenty One
Of Religious Worship, and the Sabbath Day

Confession of Faith

1. The light of nature showeth that there is a God, who hath lordship and sovereignty over all, is good, and doth good unto all, and is therefore to be feared, loved, praised, called upon, trusted in, and served, with all the heart, and with all the soul, and with all the might. But the acceptable way of worshiping the true God is instituted by himself, and so limited by his own revealed will, that he may not be worshiped according to the imaginations and devices of men, or the suggestions of Satan, under any visible representation, or any other way not prescribed in the Holy Scripture.

2. Religious worship is to be given to God, the Father, Son, and Holy Ghost; and to him alone; not to angels, saints, or any other creature: and, since the fall, not without a Mediator; nor in the mediation of any other but of Christ alone.

3. Prayer, with thanksgiving, being one special part of religious worship, is by God required of all men: and, that it may be accepted, it is to be made in the name of the Son, by the help of his Spirit, according to his will, with understanding, reverence, humility, fervency, faith, love, and perseverance; and, if vocal, in a known tongue.

4. Prayer is to be made for things lawful; and for all sorts of men living, or that shall live hereafter: but not for the dead, nor for those of whom it may be known that they have sinned the sin unto death.

5. The reading of the Scriptures with godly fear, the sound preaching and conscionable hearing of the Word, in obedience unto God, with understanding, faith, and reverence, singing of psalms with grace in the heart; as also, the due administration and worthy receiving of the sacraments instituted by Christ, are all parts of the ordinary religious worship of God: beside religious oaths, vows, solemn fastings, and thanksgivings upon special occasions, which are, in their several times and seasons, to be used in an holy

and religious manner.

6. Neither prayer, nor any other part of religious worship, is now, under the gospel, either tied unto, or made more acceptable by any place in which it is performed, or towards which it is directed: but God is to be worshiped everywhere, in spirit and truth; as, in private families daily, and in secret, each one by himself; so, more solemnly in the public assemblies, which are not carelessly or willfully to be neglected, or forsaken, when God, by his Word or providence, calleth thereunto.

7. As it is the law of nature, that, in general, a due proportion of time be set apart for the worship of God; so, in his Word, by a positive, moral, and perpetual commandment binding all men in all ages, he hath particularly appointed one day in seven, for a Sabbath, to be kept holy unto him: which, from the beginning of the world to the resurrection of Christ, was the last day of the week; and, from the resurrection of Christ, was changed into the first day of the week, which, in Scripture, is called the Lord's day, and is to be continued to the end of the world, as the Christian Sabbath.

8. This Sabbath is then kept holy unto the Lord, when men, after a due preparing of their hearts, and ordering of their common affairs beforehand, do not only observe an holy rest, all the day, from their own works, words, and thoughts about their worldly employments and recreations, but also are taken up, the whole time, in the public and private exercises of his worship, and in the duties of necessity and mercy.

THE SCRIPTURES are given to us by our Triune God to instruct us in all things pertaining to our holy faith. While there are areas of God's reality that move toward a broader perspective than set out in Scripture, there is no area that can stand except upon the foundation of Scripture. One example is mathematics. Scripture does not give us an algebraic formula; however, it does give us the principles of order and number upon which all true mathematics must stand.

There are areas in which Scripture tells us precisely what is the will of God. An example of this comes in Chapter Twenty-One of the Westminster Confession of Faith, "Of Religious Worship, and the Sabbath Day."

There are some who believe worship is such a personal matter that it should be left to the individual to decide how and when to worship God. The church has debated this down through the centuries.

What is our position within the Presbyterian Church in America? It is this: God has revealed himself in such a manner that it is obvious he is to be "feared, loved, praised, called upon, trusted in, and served, with all the heart, and with all the soul, and with all the might" (paragraph one).

However, the same paragraph specifies that God can be truly worshiped only according to Scripture. Our position is that God has not left worship to our imaginations. We are to worship him according to knowledge, and we receive that knowledge in Scripture alone.

This was the focus of the historic debate between the Lutheran and Reformed members of the Protestant family. The Lutheran position affirms that one can use anything in worship not specifically forbidden by Scripture, whereas our position is that we are free to use only those elements of worship instituted by God.

Holding to this does not mean that we are forced to say, as some groups have maintained, that there can be no choir or musical instruments in worship. Nor does it require exclusive Psalm singing. We are not simply New Testament or Old Testament Christians; our faith is the biblical faith—Old and New Testaments. Do you recall two Old Testament incidents when God was worshiped contrary to his will and became angry? One was in Genesis 4 and involved Cain and Abel. The other was in Deuteronomy 9, when the Hebrews worshiped a golden calf. In both instances, worship was contrary to God's way and God reacted with judgment.

This chapter of the confession underscores that we are worshiping the Triune God alone. No angel worship. No ancestry worship. No creature worship of any kind. We worship the Father, the Son, and the Holy Ghost, and because of our sinfulness our worship must be through the Mediator, Jesus Christ. He is our way to God. There is no other. See John 14:6; 2 Timothy 2:5.

What is acceptable worship of God? Whatever we decide? No! Only what God sets forth in his Word.

As you study the development of Christian doctrine, you may come across the expression "regulative principle of worship." It means that the parts of our worship of God are regulated by his Word.

The confession cites those elements commanded and authorized by Scripture. Read paragraphs three, four, five, and six for details. But a summary of the elements of worship that please God would begin with **prayer**. Prayer is regulated by the Word of God. However, while it is good at times to recite the prayers of the Bible, God does not hold us to that in all praying. Yet even in verbalizing our prayers, the Word of God in Scripture must be our guide. There are some things lawful for prayer, and some things unlawful.

There is a right way and a wrong way to pray. The Bible guides us in the right way, which helps us to pray in accordance with God's will. Scripture helps us to pray and others to pray freely with us in worship by praying in a "known tongue" (paragraph three). There is nothing hidden, esoteric, or superstitiously mystical about our prayers. They simply communicate with God in accordance with his revealed will.

We are to pray for his will to be done and for sinners to be converted; however, we do not pray for those who have committed the "sin that leads to death" (1 John 5:16).

In true worship there is "**the reading of Scriptures** with godly fear." The Scriptures, according to Chapter One, are to be in the language of the people, from a faithful translation. This element is not to be replaced with the reading of someone's paraphrase of the Scriptures. There may be a place for that but not to replace the reading of Scripture.

The Word is to be soundly preached. A proper exposition from the Word is essential to true worship. It cannot be replaced with concerts, programs, and films. There is a place for those things in the life of the church, but when they replace the sound preaching, they destroy true worship. Any discourse that is not faithful to Scripture undermines true worship.

Those Christians in churches that have substituted liberal humanism, dialogues, and other forms of worship for sound preaching need to look carefully at what the true worship of God really involves.

The people must listen to the Word of God, read and preached, with the intention to hear, understand, and obey. This generates reverence, understanding, and faith. If our intention in worship is not to hear and obey God's Word, then we jeopardize an acceptable worship before God.

The sacraments of baptism and the Lord's Supper are to be rightly administered and received in a worthy manner. The church cannot make the sacraments optional, nor can the church administer them in any other manner than that prescribed in Scripture. You will recall that the proper administration of the sacraments was one of the rediscovered true marks of the church during the Protestant Reformation.

The confession speaks of other exercises and other occasions for worship in paragraph five. We merely call them to your attention.

As to the time and place of worship, paragraphs six, seven, and eight have some instructions that are helpful. Particularly do we call attention to paragraph eight. While there is to be freedom in worship, and we should worship the Lord every day, the Christian Sabbath calls our attention to the necessity of regular public worship. God's law says, "Remember the Sabbath Day by keeping it holy" (Ex. 20:8). That's the Christian's day of public worship together.

Properly observed, the Christian Sabbath is our delight and not our burden. It crystallizes and epitomizes all true worship of God. Examine your worship of God. Is it consistent with his Word? What are you omitting? Are there things that you do and call worship that are not set forth in Scripture? How do you pray? What do you pray for? What do you neglect in prayer? Is the Christian Sabbath your special day of covenant family worship, fellowship, and rest?

You would benefit from a study of Chapter Twenty-One and from the book, *Discovering the Fullness of Worship*, by Paul Engle, a Great Commission Publications study. They will help you to understand and practice true scriptural worship.

Chapter Twenty Two

Of Lawful Oaths and Vows

CONFESSION OF FAITH

1. A lawful oath is a part of religious worship, wherein, upon just occasion, the person swearing solemnly calleth God to witness what he asserteth, or promiseth, and to judge him according to the truth or falsehood of what he sweareth.

2. The name of God only is that by which men ought to swear, and therein it is to be used with all holy fear and reverence. Therefore, to swear vainly, or rashly, by that glorious and dreadful Name; or, to swear at all by any other thing, is sinful, and to be abhorred. Yet, as in matters of weight and moment, an oath is warranted by the Word of God, under the new testament as well as under the old; so a lawful oath, being imposed by lawful authority, in such matters, ought to be taken.

3. Whosoever taketh an oath ought duly to consider the weightiness of so solemn an act, and therein to avouch nothing but what he is fully persuaded is the truth: neither may any man bind himself by oath to anything but what is good and just, and what he believeth so to be, and what he is able and resolved to perform.

4. An oath is to be taken in the plain and common sense of the words, without equivocation, or mental reservation. It cannot oblige to sin; but in anything not sinful, being taken, it binds to performance, although to a man's own hurt. Nor is it to be violated, although made to heretics, or infidels.

5. A vow is of the like nature with a promissory oath, and ought to be made with the like religious care, and to be performed with the like faithfulness.

6. It is not to be made to any creature, but to God alone: and, that it may be accepted, it is to be made voluntarily, out of faith, and conscience of duty, in way of thankfulness for mercy received, or for the obtaining of what we want, whereby we more strictly bind ourselves to necessary duties; or, to other things, so far and so long as they may fitly conduce thereunto.

7. No man may vow to do anything forbidden in the Word of God, or what would hinder any duty therein commanded, or which is not in his own power, and for the performance whereof he hath no promise of ability from God. In which respects, popish monastical vows of perpetual single life, professed poverty, and regular obedience, are so far from being degrees of higher perfection, that they are superstitious and sinful snares, in which no Christian may entangle himself.

CHRISTIANS, above all people, should have the reputation of possessing the fullest integrity. Our word should be our bond. As followers of the true God, we are to be known as people who represent truth. Unfortunately, such is not always the case.

The tongue can be and often is a deadly enemy within the Christian community. We speak when we should be listening. Or we forget to guard carefully against the danger of our presuppositions that we often color issues and distort them. Or we pride ourselves in speaking the truth but do not speak it in love. Or we speak for the wrong reasons or at the wrong time. We do much damage.

This chapter in the Westminster Confession of Faith, "Of Lawful Oaths and Vows," could easily be labeled "the chapter on the tongue." Its content reflects once again that the confession does not deal only with abstracts but also with concrete, real-life situations. It answers questions that are frequently raised: Should I take an oath? Do I really have to swear?

True, there are false or minced oaths—perversions of the true oath. True, in heaven we will have no need of oaths. But until then let us understand what Scripture says about this matter. First, we are told in this chapter of the confession, paragraph one, that "a lawful oath is part of religious worship, wherein, upon just occasion, the person swearing solemnly calleth God to witness what he answereth or promiseth, and to judge him according to the truth or falsehood of what he sweareth."

We read in Deuteronomy 10:20 that Moses was instructed to swear in the name of the Lord. This idea is also present in the New Testament, where Paul called on God for a witness (2 Cor. 1:23).

But what about Matthew 5:33–37? Doesn't it teach us not to swear or make an oath? Such a reading reflects a removal of that passage from the context. Christ is underscoring the importance of speaking the truth and the deadliness of speaking lies. Christians should let their yea be yea and their nay, nay. They should never give anyone reason to question their integrity. They should speak the truth without having to swear by an oath.

It was the flippant oath to which Jesus referred. This kind is not necessary, and becomes profanity, which has no place in the Christian's life.

When we make an assertion or a promise, it should be in the name of God, which indicates that what we have said is true. God is my witness. No other person or thing, real or imaginary, counts. Only the name of God. It has to be in his name, though it may be imposed on us by lawful authorities or at our own initiative.

All through the Bible we find God's warning to those who perjure themselves or swear deceitfully. God warns against saying one thing and meaning another. For example: a person who takes certain vows; a minister who vows to hold to certain beliefs but does not do so; a church officer who is required to hold to a certain doctrine and discipline but does not do so intentionally.

Oath taking is a serious matter. Remember this when you are called to take vows, whether it be as a minister, officer, father, husband, wife, etc. We who fall into the above categories have in fact taken vows. God is the witness to our integrity. Nothing can be hidden from God.

The confession warns against taking oaths that are not good and just. It encourages taking an oath on anything that is good and just, when imposed by lawful authorities. The reference is to civil matters and church membership, but it also has implications for the home.

We should not hesitate or equivocate when asked to take an oath, even if it is before unbelievers. Paragraph four deals with this aspect. A vow binds us to performance even when it may hurt our own interests. A man's word must be taken seriously.

This is also why paragraph five warns us to make our oaths and vows with religious care. We have to do what we vow to do. If it is a promissory oath, we must do it. If it is an assertion, it must be true.

Be careful, warns the confession, about taking vows that are not in keeping with Scripture. The last paragraph gives examples of such vows.

Keeping in mind the historical context of the confession in stating the Protestant views over against those of Roman Catholicism, Rome required monastic vows of a perpetual single life, professed poverty, and regular obedience. Stay away from all religious vows that attempt to bind your conscience with an oath, when those vows are not biblically founded.

The Roman Catholic Church is not the only religious group that uses the name of Christ for things that are not scriptural. Some twentieth-century cults and sects are as deadly in such requirements. The confession, echoing the voice of Scripture, says no Christian should ever make a vow or take an oath lightly.

Gordon Clark uses this example: "One may vow to walk around the block five times for the next five days as an expression of thanksgiving to God for the gift of good health. Such a vow when taken, should be observed with scrupulous care; but there are better ways to thank God for health. If one forms a habit of making foolish vows, it is more likely that spiritual decay will set in" (*What Do Presbyterians Believe?*, 205).

Let your yea be yea and your nay, nay. Do not place yourself under the unbiblical practices of any religious group. When you take an oath or make a vow, keep it.

Chapter Twenty Three

OF THE CIVIL MAGISTRATE

CONFESSION OF FAITH

1. God, the supreme Lord and King of all the world, hath ordained civil magistrates, to be, under him, over the people, for his own glory, and the public good: and, to this end, hath armed them with the power of the sword, for the defense and encouragement of them that are good, and for the punishment of evildoers.

2. It is lawful for Christians to accept and execute the office of a magistrate, when called thereunto: in the managing whereof, as they ought especially to maintain piety, justice, and peace, according to the wholesome laws of each commonwealth; so, for that end, they may lawfully, now under the new testament, wage war, upon just and necessary occasion.

3. Civil magistrates may not assume to themselves the administration of the Word and sacraments; or the power of the keys of the kingdom of heaven; or, in the least, interfere in matters of faith. Yet, as nursing fathers, it is the duty of civil magistrates to protect the church of our common Lord, without giving the preference to any denomination of Christians above the rest, in such a manner that all ecclesiastical persons whatever shall enjoy the full, free, and unquestioned liberty of discharging every part of their sacred functions, without violence or danger. And, as Jesus Christ hath appointed a regular government and discipline in his church, no law of any commonwealth should interfere with, let, or hinder, the due exercise thereof, among the voluntary members of any denomination of Christians, according to their own profession and belief. It is the duty of civil magistrates to protect the person and good name of all their people, in such an effectual manner as that no person be suffered, either upon pretense of religion or of infidelity, to offer any indignity, violence, abuse, or injury to any other person whatsoever: and to take order, that all religious and ecclesiastical assemblies be held without molestation or disturbance.

4.   It is the duty of people to pray for magistrates, to honor their persons, to pay them tribute or other dues, to obey their lawful commands, and to be subject to their authority, for conscience' sake. Infidelity, or difference in religion, doth not make void the magistrates' just and legal authority, nor free the people from their due obedience to them: from which ecclesiastical persons are not exempted, much less hath the pope any power and jurisdiction over them in their dominions, or over any of their people; and, least of all, to deprive them of their dominions, or lives, if he shall judge them to be heretics, or upon any other pretense whatsoever.

WHO WOULD SAY, after careful reading, that the Westminster Confession of Faith does not deal with real-life issues? Chapter Twenty-Three deals with one of the most important contemporary problems that confront Christians. The role of the state (civil authorities) and the responsibility of Christians in the political arena are two of the most talked-about topics. Christians, religious leaders, politicians, and organizations such as the American Civil Liberties Union are frequently debating this issue.

Political activity of the 1980s, both within the church and beyond to the civil realm, forced Christians to deal with the role of the civil magistrate and the responsibility of Christians.

In election years, citizens of the United States go to the polls to vote. Is there a Christian view of politics set forth in Scripture that Christians should reflect?

This chapter is outstandingly practical in its teaching. The chapter is one in which the United States edition of the confession differs with the original 1647 edition. Here is what our confession states:

1.   Civil magistrates are ordained by God. He has given to them the power of the sword. He has not given them sovereign power. That belongs only to God. Their power is derived from him, and it is a ministerial power.

   Paragraph one reads like a paraphrase of Romans 13:1–7, and that it is: civil authorities are ordained by God and armed with limited authority.

   They exist for the glory of God and the good of the people.

105

They have been given authority (symbolized by the sword) to defend and encourage those who are good, and they have a God-given mandate to punish evildoers.

God set up the positions and job descriptions for the civil authorities. He did it for his glory and our good. He did not develop a specific form of government, except that all government should be theocratic, i.e., ruled by God. Wherever we find ourselves on earth, the powers that be are ordained by God.

Though some forms of government may be better than others, a representative-type government seems to be more closely aligned with Scripture (elected leaders who represent God and the people in the areas of defense and justice).

2.   **Paragraph two** answers common questions. Should Christians be involved in politics? May Christians hold political office? Paragraph two says, "It is lawful for Christians to accept and execute the office of a magistrate [civil authority] when called thereunto." It is a calling similar to that within the church realm.

When Christians are called to political office, it is incumbent on them "to maintain piety, justice, and peace, according to the wholesome laws of each commonwealth." As citizens we live in two realms. We do not resign our political responsibilities just because we are Christians.

Christians should seek public office in order to promote the things spelled out in paragraph two. Paragraphs one and two state two very important points: the state can and must punish evildoers, and the state can and must wage just war.

The modern emphasis on criminals not being punished and wars not being waged is at odds with biblical teaching. God's Word demands that evildoers be punished. It also gives examples of just wars.

Our young people especially need instruction in this area of the confession and the biblical teaching from which the confession was written. So much needs to be said about these points. For now, we simply underscore the right and responsibility of the civil authorities in regard to crime and war.

3. The **third paragraph** makes that all-important distinction in rendering unto Caesar the things that are Caesar's, and unto God the things that are God's. It is one of the best statements in the English language on church and state separation. What it says is this:

    The state must not usurp the duties of the church, i.e., preaching the gospel and administering the sacraments. It must not interfere with any matters of faith.

    What about legal disputes between Christians? Paul says in 1 Corinthians 6:1–6 that Christians should bring lawsuits against Christians.

    However, the state is responsible to protect God's ordained institutions, and the church is one of these. The state must protect the church "as nursing fathers" protect their children, the confession teaches. However, the state must not give preference to one denomination above others.

    If it does, it has overstepped its bounds, and charges could be made against it. Such preference would violate the freedom of individuals to follow their own consciences. Notice that the wording does not prohibit assistance to religion, for the United States was founded to be a Christian nation, but it does prohibit favored treatment of a denomination. We are to have no state church. Civil authorities must see to it that we do not.

    The state authorities also must protect the rights of individuals to meet in ecclesiastical assemblies without "molestation or disturbance."

    The responsibility of the state is twofold: one, to protect the church as an institution from civil persecution; two, to protect individuals and see that they have the right to freedom of assembly where church life is concerned.

4. What are the duties of Christian people to the civil authorities? Paragraph four spells out several: one, we are duty-bound to pray

for the leaders (1 Tim. 2:1–2); two, we are to pay them tribute and other dues (1 Peter 2:17; Rom. 13:6–7); three, we are to obey their lawful commands and be subject to their authority for conscience sake (Rom. 13:5; Titus 3:1). Notice the use of the word *lawful* in regard to commands. Obviously, our first allegiance is to God. The state cannot command our conscience, but God can. If there is ever a choice (God forbid) of our allegiance to God or to the state, then the state forfeits its right to our Christian duties. When the state begins to ban the Christian religion from state-supported and state-established institutions, it treads on dangerous ground. It may forfeit its right to the people's prayers, honor, tribute, and submission.

However, what if a non-Christian is elected to office? What if the officeholder is an adherent of another religion or even denies any religious profession? We are still to give him his honor, his due, and our prayers. Remember that Paul wrote his instruction to Christians living under pagan Roman authority.

Is this not a timely subject? In too many instances now our national, state, and local leaders have taken from us the freedom guaranteed in the Constitution of the United States.

Christians must know the issues. They must be able to give a reason for their positions and set forth their case. We cannot allow our nation to serve Caesar with unlimited power. We must not put people into office who represent anything less than what is set forth in Chapter Twenty-Three.

Have you developed a political philosophy in keeping with Scripture and this doctrine? Will it be reflected in your rights and privileges as voting citizens of this republic?

Chapter Twenty Four
OF MARRIAGE AND DIVORCE

CONFESSION OF FAITH

1. Marriage is to be between one man and one woman: neither is it lawful for any man to have more than one wife, nor for any woman to have more than one husband, at the same time.

2. Marriage was ordained for the mutual help of husband and wife, for the increase of mankind with legitimate issue, and of the church with an holy seed; and for preventing of uncleanness.

3. It is lawful for all sorts of people to marry, who are able with judgment to give their consent. Yet it is the duty of Christians to marry only in the Lord. And therefore such as profess the true reformed religion should not marry with infidels, papists, or other idolaters: neither should such as are godly be unequally yoked, by marrying with such as are notoriously wicked in their life, or maintain damnable heresies.

4. Marriage ought not to be within the degrees of consanguinity or affinity forbidden by the Word. Nor can such incestuous marriages ever be made lawful by any law of man or consent of parties, so as those persons may live together as man and wife.

5. Adultery or fornication committed after a contract, being detected before marriage, giveth just occasion to the innocent party to dissolve that contract. In the case of adultery after marriage, it is lawful for the innocent party to sue out a divorce: and, after the divorce, to marry another, as if the offending party were dead.

6. Although the corruption of man be such as is apt to study arguments unduly to put asunder those whom God hath joined together in marriage: yet, nothing but adultery, or such willful desertion as can no way be remedied by the church, or civil magistrate, is cause sufficient of dissolving the bond of marriage: wherein, a public and orderly course of proceeding is to be

observed; and the persons concerned in it not left to their own wills, and discretion, in their own case.

JUST AS the confession's Chapter Twenty-Three dealt with a contemporary subject, the political realm, so Chapter Twenty-Four deals with a topic of considerable current interest. It is about marriage and divorce, and teachings about them that are so often misunderstood and misapplied in today's society.

Many people's lives have been wrecked not only by problems of marriage and divorce, but also by misunderstanding of God's will in regard to them. Some have gone to the extreme of saying that there are no rules at all, that anything goes. Others have gone in the opposite direction and maintained that the rules are so fixed that marriage or divorce is not allowed.

Aware of one extreme or another, some people live under a load of guilt, which may or may not have a biblical basis. It may be false guilt instead of real guilt. We need to know the difference from the Bible since Scripture, properly interpreted, is the final authority in all religious matters (Chapter One, paragraph ten).

This chapter of the confession deals with six major aspects of marriage and divorce.

First, marriage is monogamous. A man should not have more than one wife or a woman more than one husband at the same time. Though polygamy was practiced in Old Testament times and though some cultures practice it today, God's purpose in marriage was monogamy: one husband and one wife. The phrase "at the same time" in the first paragraph is significant. Remarriage is possible for Christians, and in most cases desirable, when biblical conditions are met.

Second, we learn in Genesis 2:18–25 that God ordained the marriage institution. He established marriage. "The LORD God said, 'It is not good for the man to be alone. I will make a helper suitable for him'" (Gen. 2:18).

Jay Adams uses a term that expresses both the unity and diversity of marriage. The unifying concept is that it is a "covenant of companionship" ("for the mutual help of husband and wife," paragraph two says.). This is the basic reason for marriage.

Growing out of that covenant, marriage meets a diversity of needs. A husband and wife need to enjoy an intimate relationship with each other. Such a relationship has physical and spiritual ramifications, inner belonging, and sexual satisfaction.

Another need met by the institution of marriage is to provide for children. This does not suggest that there can be no proper marriage without children, and we know that many children are born to unwed parents. Yet God's way is through marriage. Children are to be born within that institution. The wording of the second paragraph underscores the importance of children, not only to the marriage institution but also to the church. Replenishing the earth was one of God's original creation ordinances.

Third, the confession deals with eligibility for marriage. Paragraph three says, "It is lawful for all sorts of people to marry . . ." Marriage is a legal institution for all kinds of people. It is not reserved for one race or blood.

However, the confession, following Scripture, does set down some specifications. What are they? The main one is that each man and woman must be "able with judgment to give their consent." The implication is that it is a voluntary covenant, but once made it carries many stipulations and requirements.

Christians are "only to marry in the Lord. And therefore such as profess the true reformed religion should not marry with infidels, papists, and other idolaters: neither should such as are godly be unequally yoked, by marrying with such as are notoriously wicked in their life, or maintain damnable heresies." Believers in the Lord should only marry believers in the Lord. Elsewhere, the Bible has something to say about the marriage of two unbelievers where one is converted later, and what those requirements are.

Fourth, another stipulation is that one cannot marry within the same bloodline relationship. In the original version of the confession there is an added statement prohibiting a man's marriage with any of his wife's close kin and vice versa. (See Lev. 18.) Without giving a detailed explanation here, this difference in the original version and the PCA version is noted. Most other American editions drop that statement also.

Fifth, the last two paragraphs deal with divorce and related matters. The text underscores on the one hand that God does hate divorce (Mal. 2:16). His will for marriage is that it is a covenant "till death do us part." However, as he had to do with Israel because of her sin (Jer. 3:8), so does he set up the criteria for divorce.

The Bible and the confession take engagement very seriously and establish one ground for breaking an engagement contract. It is adultery or sexual immorality before consummation of the marriage.

Marriage is dissolved by death, but until then there are only two biblical grounds for divorce. They are adultery and "such willful desertion as can no way be remedied by the church, or civil magistrate . . . ." The confession carefully follows Scripture at this point, and so must we. Today there are those who claim there are no biblical grounds for divorce, while others claim there are no limitations on divorce.

God, who established marriage, is also the one who revealed his will regarding divorce. This chapter's fifth and sixth paragraphs are excellent summaries of the teaching of God's Word on this subject. We need this material in the confession because positions contrary to the Bible are held so often and because nearly any discussion of marriage, divorce, and remarriage carries many emotional overtones.

We Christians need to be sensitive to those who have had their lives scarred and marred by broken marriages. We need to exercise deep sensitivity and a Christlike attitude as we seek to give counsel to such people.

Limited space does not permit a full discussion of such a complex matter. However, two excellent books are available that deal with it from the perspective of the Confession of Faith. One is *Divorce*, by John Murray. The other, *Marriage and Divorce*, by Jay Adams, is newer, and in our judgment the best. Both should be read, but especially the latter.

Chapter Twenty Five
Of the Church (Part One)

Confession of Faith

1. The catholic or universal church, which is invisible, consists of the whole number of the elect, that have been, are, or shall be gathered into one, under Christ the Head thereof; and is the spouse, the body, the fullness of him that filleth all in all.

2. The visible church, which is also catholic or universal under the gospel (not confined to one nation, as before under the law), consists of all those throughout the world that profess the true religion; and of their children: and is the kingdom of the Lord Jesus Christ, the house and family of God, out of which there is no ordinary possibility of salvation.

3. Unto this catholic visible church Christ hath given the ministry, oracles, and ordinances of God, for the gathering and perfecting of the saints, in this life, to the end of the world: and doth, by his own presence and Spirit, according to his promise, make them effectual thereunto.

4. This catholic church hath been sometimes more, sometimes less visible. And particular churches, which are members thereof, are more or less pure, according as the doctrine of the gospel is taught and embraced, ordinances administered, and public worship performed more or less purely in them.

5. The purest churches under heaven are subject both to mixture and error; and some have so degenerated, as to become no churches of Christ, but synagogues of Satan. Nevertheless, there shall be always a church on earth, to worship God according to his will.

6. There is no other head of the church but the Lord Jesus Christ. Nor can the pope of Rome, in any sense, be head thereof.

IF EVER there were a deficient view of the church, it is the view widely held today. In the Bible the word "church" is not a fuzzy term, but something definite and concrete. The deficiency is seen in both extremes of liberal and fundamentalist Christianity.

There is an obvious misunderstanding in people's minds today regarding what the church of Jesus Christ is and what relationship Christians have with the church. Though Chapter Twenty-Five is not an exhaustive treatise on the doctrine of the church, it does deal with several aspects that are essential for our understanding.

We shall consider this chapter in two parts. This summary will contain part one. It will deal with the church as God sees it and relates to it.

First, the Apostles' Creed, which comes to us from the early church, contains the phrase "we believe in the holy catholic church." Paragraph one of Chapter Twenty-Five begins with the terminology, "the catholic or universal Church." The term "catholic church" often confuses contemporary ears. It sounds like the Roman Catholic Church, but that is not meant here. The confession's use of the word "catholic" is qualified by the word "universal." The church of the Lord Jesus Christ is the universal church. It is not confined to one people or one place, but is a worldwide entity.

Second, the confession states that the universal church is invisible. In paragraph two we shall also observe that it is described as the visible church. You may have read about the church militant and the church triumphant, or the church as an organism and the church as an organization. At this time in history ("HIS-story") the church is both visible and invisible. Being invisible certainly is not a reference to God's inability to see the church. He sees all things. It must have reference to man, who is a creature of time and space.

The word "invisible" draws our attention to the fact that the church is a spiritual organism in her essence and cannot be seen with the physical eye. Humanly we cannot clearly know who is and isn't a true part of that organism. Only God knows. In that respect the church is invisible. She is also invisible in the sense that she is universal, and we cannot see the whole church. She is a worldwide spiritual organism.

Third, the church consists "of the whole number of the elect, that have been, are, or shall be gathered into one, under Christ the Head thereof . . . ."

114

Again this phrase describes those who comprise the invisible church of Jesus Christ. Chapter Three of the confession deals extensively with statements defining the elect.

Fourth, the church is "the spouse, the body, the fullness of Him that filleth all in all." This is good New Testament terminology. The church is the bride of Christ. The church is the body of Christ.

Such descriptive terminology immediately reminds us of the close organic relationship that the church has with the Lord. Obviously these words suggest the closest and the most personal relationship.

Fifth, the church is also visible. It "consists of all those throughout the world that profess the true religion; and of their children . . . ." Keep in mind that the invisible aspect of the church combines those true believers now on earth and those in heaven. The visible church refers to those on earth now, with their children, who profess the true religion.

Here is where we must take a serious look at our understanding of the church and our relationship to it. This has been distorted and perverted down through the years. For example: Roman Catholicism tends to emphasize that the church is essential for salvation, that there is no salvation outside the church—though the Vatican II Council of the 1950s and 1960s has moderated this once-absolute position. But the Roman Catholic Church still seems to equate joining the visible church with being saved. Some fundamentalist groups today do the same thing and indicate that unless you belong to their particular church you cannot be saved. There is no biblical validity to such a position—after all, there was only one church in the first thousand years.

On the other hand, there is an equally dangerous position abroad that maintains one can be a good Christian, saved, and sanctified, and not belong to the visible church. Some modern parachurch movements are guilty of such direction. Often it is not an overt emphasis, but it surfaces at times.

Many professing Christians have no relationship to the visible church today; and yet they believe they are honoring God. The confession concludes paragraph two with wording that reflects the Bible's emphasis. It states that ordinarily there is no salvation outside the visible church. What does that mean, and why such wording? The words "ordinary possibility of salvation" refer to the way a person is normally saved. The church preaches the Word, and people are saved and joined to the visible church, if not already related.

The visible church is defined as those who profess true faith and their children.

However, "ordinary possibility of salvation" keeps before us the danger of Roman Catholicism's error. There are undoubtedly some rare exceptions where one has been converted and could not join the visible church: the penitent thief on the cross, a deathbed conversion, and the like.

Normally, one cannot be a faithful Christian and remain invisible or out of the body. Becoming a Christian and professing the true religion identifies one with the spiritual organism and physical organization called the church.

In the next section we shall consider which visible church we should join. Joining the visible church is not an option for the Christian, but he does have the freedom to choose a particular church.

The sacraments belong to the church, and Christians are to receive the sacraments. They are to be administered, not privately, but by the visible church. The confession also describes the visible church as "the kingdom of the Lord Jesus Christ, the house and family of God."

Some American churches have added to this description of the visible church, but the Presbyterian Church in America has chosen to stay with the original wording at this point.

In the next section we shall consider the remaining paragraphs of Chapter Twenty-Five. Because the church is the bride of Christ and the body of Christ, we who profess to be Christians must maintain a high and holy view of the church. Our membership must not be considered an optional relationship. John Calvin wrote that he who has God for his father would have the church for his mother.

Understanding this truth will keep you from the extremes of saying that church membership saves, or maintaining that the church is optional for Christians.

Chapter Twenty Five
Of the Church (Part Two)

THE ROLE of the church in the building of God's kingdom is indispensable. The Westminster Confession of Faith, Chapter Twenty-Five, helps in understanding what the church is and what mission she has been given by the King and Head of the church, Jesus Christ.

Paragraphs one and two (discussed above) deal with the nature and scope of the church. By summary, it is the body of God's elect throughout the world. Belonging to the church—God's family—is extremely important, as paragraph two states. **Paragraph three** explains why.

"Unto this catholic visible Church Christ hath given the ministry, oracles, and ordinances of God, for the gathering and perfecting of the saints, in this life, to the end of the world . . . ." In Ephesians 4:12, Paul says that the primary mission of the church is to equip the saints for the building of his body.

The church is the cradle that holds the Word and the sacraments. She is the mother who nourishes her children with those ingredients. She is the holder of the keys to God's kingdom.

The church has the responsibility of distributing the Word and the sacraments. She cannot make them effectual but she must distribute them. To this end God has given his presence and Spirit to make that ministry effectual. Think of the church like this: God's people, gathered around his Word and sacraments, with God in the midst to bless and to make disciples through the ministry of those elements.

Throughout the history of God's people from the Garden of Eden to this day, there has always been the church. However, at times the church has been more visible than at other times (**paragraph four**). You can trace this throughout history. There were periods in Old Testament times when the body of believers was not as visible as at other times. The period before the coming of Christ was one of those less-visible times.

Prior to the Reformation and during the Dark Ages, the visible church was hardly seen, at least the biblical visible church. She had ceased to be a faithful dispenser of the Word and sacraments; yet the church was not extinguished. When God builds his church the gates of hell cannot prevail against her, as Jesus reminded the disciples.

At times particular churches (locally and denominationally) are less pure and do not properly minister the Word and the sacraments. Public worship has at times been perverted and hurt the church's witness—examples being the church at Corinth in Paul's day and the Roman Church of the Dark Ages. Though the examples are different, they both reflect adverse consequences for the church's ministry when she does not fulfill her God-given mission.

Yet, God used Paul to deal with Corinth. He used Luther, Calvin, and others to bring about a Reformation within his church. The Protestant Reformation was a movement that brought new visibility to God's church. It was out of this backdrop that our own Presbyterian Church in America was formed. The PCA was formed by men who believed the marks of a true church were not as visible in their mother church as God would have them be. Dr. Morton Smith's book, *How Is the Gold Become Dim*, was written to address this point."

Paragraph five reminds us that even the "purest Churches under heaven are subject both to mixture and error; and some have so degenerated as to become no Churches of Christ, but synagogues of Satan." Several things distinguish a faithful church. The Reformers cited three marks of a true church: true biblical preaching, proper observance of church discipline, and correct administration of the sacraments.

Read the last sentence in paragraph five. A word of encouragement is always helpful. What happens when a church loses her marks and God removes his lampstand from that church (locally or denominationally)? "Nevertheless, there shall be always a Church on earth to worship God according to His will." Though one church defaults and loses its true marks, there will always be a remnant, a visible church on earth. You see this in the cyclical flow of church history from Eden to this day. There is a remnant. God is never left without witness; neither are God's people left without the church, even in such hard times as first-century Egypt and

Rome, sixteenth-century Europe, and modern America.

These words remind us of several great hymns used in worship. A stanza in Martin Luther's "A Mighty Fortress Is Our God" affirms, "And though this world with devils filled, should threaten to undo us, we will not fear, for God hath willed His truth to triumph through us."

The confession both reminds us and encourages us that there will always be a church on earth.

Last, the **sixth paragraph** was worded to speak to a particular issue of the era when the confession was framed, but the principle is true for all times. The pope of the Church of Rome was both claiming to be and given the honor of being the head of the church. The Reformers even referred to him as the anti-Christ, and certainly as he or any other would usurp Christ's place, he was the embodiment of the anti-Christ principle.

Therefore, the text includes these words: "There is no other head of the Church but the Lord Jesus Christ. Nor can the Pope of Rome, in any sense, be head thereof."

No one has the right to take Christ's place in his church. The vicar of Rome dishonors the Lord when he allows himself to be revered as the head of the church.

The modern cult leaders who claim a similar role are to be immediately recognized and exposed as those embodying the anti-Christ principle. There is only one true head of the church, Jesus Christ.

It is most appropriate that the PCA's Book of Church Order (government) includes the early statement affirming Christ's headship and the church's responsibility to carry out his will. We must work and pray to keep his church as pure as we can by carrying out our mission of equipping the saints, then moving into the world with the gospel message.

We must denounce any attempt to pervert the church's ministry and dethrone Christ's authority. We must also be equipped to know how to deal with the twentieth-century phenomenon that implies membership in the visible church is optional.

Last, we must self-consciously involve ourselves in the ministry of the Lord Jesus Christ in building up his body, the church. This is to be done within the context of the visible church, whose mission is to dispense the ministry, oracles, and ordinances of God.

Chapter Twenty Six
OF THE COMMUNION OF SAINTS

CONFESSION OF FAITH

1. All saints, that are united to Jesus Christ their Head, by his Spirit, and by faith, have fellowship with him in his graces, sufferings, death, resurrection, and glory: and, being united to one another in love, they have communion in each other's gifts and graces, and are obliged to the performance of such duties, public and private, as do conduce to their mutual good, both in the inward and outward man.

2. Saints by profession are bound to maintain an holy fellowship and communion in the worship of God, and in performing such other spiritual services as tend to their mutual edification; as also in relieving each other in outward things, according to their several abilities and necessities. Which communion, as God offereth opportunity, is to be extended unto all those who, in every place, call upon the name of the Lord Jesus.

3. This communion which the saints have with Christ, doth not make them in any wise partakers of the substance of his Godhead; or to be equal with Christ in any respect: either of which to affirm is impious and blasphemous. Nor doth their communion one with another, as saints, take away, or infringe the title or propriety which each man hath in his goods and possessions.

THIS CHAPTER of the Westminster Confession of Faith strikes at the very heart of an issue that continues to plague the church today in many areas. That is the misunderstanding of what being a Christian really is.

What is the misunderstanding? Isn't it simple enough to say that a Christian is a person who is related to God through Christ on a one-to-one basis? Actually, such a statement is too simplistic and has the ring of misconception, if it is all that is said.

The whole truth from Scripture would lead us to say that a Christian is a person who is personally related to God through Christ and who is also in real union with other believers. Is this what the Scriptures really teach?

Absolutely! To be joined to Christ by faith is also to be joined to his body. Remember that in the previous chapter on the church how the writers were careful to maintain that salvation is ordinarily not possible outside the church, the body?

Say it like this: Christianity is both individualistic and covenantal. It is not either/or; it is both/and. You cannot have Christ the Lord as your Savior apart from the body of which he is the head.

When we say, as many do each Sunday in reciting the Apostles' Creed, that we believe in the "communion of saints," do we understand what we are saying? Chapter Twenty-Six is a precise commentary on that point. Let's examine it:

First, "All saints, that are joined to Jesus Christ their Head, by His spirit, and by faith, have fellowship with Him in His graces, sufferings, death, resurrection, and glory . . . ." Any edition of the confession with Scripture texts will give you a number of citations that deal with this.

By faith we are joined to him in fellowship. However, as paragraph three underscores, this does not mean we have become partakers in his deity or incommunicable attributes. This union does not make us equal with Christ in any respect. It is a spiritual union experienced and appropriated by faith.

He is and remains the creator God. We are always his creation. We never rise above that status. Even as saints (believers), we are still creatures of his hand.

We are not of the same stuff as God. To maintain that we are or that we are somehow equal with God is both "impious and blasphemous" (paragraph three).

He is the vine, we are the branches (John 15:5). He is the head; we are the body (Col. 1:18). This is a mystical union brought about by God's grace through faith.

Second, once we are joined to Christ by faith as the vine or head, we are joined to one another in love and have communion with each other's gifts and graces (paragraph one).

If we have a living relationship with the Lord, there grows out of that relationship a living union with all who are "in Christ." First Corinthians

12–14, Ephesians 4, Colossians 1:18 underscore both the horizontal and vertical aspects of union with God and one another. Neither the horizontal nor the vertical is optional. Both are vital, and ordinarily neither can be separated from the other.

What this implies is that we are not independent of God or of one another. While we could say that God the head could exist apart from the body because he is self-sufficient, we of the body are not alive apart from him and are in bad trouble if we try to deny our relationship to the body. We are not self-sufficient.

The confession makes it clear that just as union with God involves privileges and responsibilities, so does our union with others. However, how far do we take this? Do I forfeit all my rights?

No! Paragraph three makes clear that this union with other believers does not destroy our right to titles and property, that is, goods and possessions. Though there have been times from Acts 2:44 until this day when certain Christians have pooled all their goods, such is neither re-quired nor commanded.

Then what does it mean? We have a responsibility both in private and public to perform those acts that are conducive to the good of other believers, both in the inward and outward man.

As one reads the second paragraph, this instruction is fairly obvious. Communion involves our duties to attend church and worship together. It involves joint praise, prayer, and stewardship: meeting the needs of one another physically and spiritually according to our abilities and necessities.

The confession also refers to an attitude of giving and receiving. Christians should know both how to give and how to receive, how to share a burden and how to bear a burden. We cannot ignore the duty to serve one another.

Often God's way of ministering to us is through fellow Christians. All through the Bible we find believers being built up by the ministry and concern of others.

This is a responsibility and privilege for all believers who call on the name of the Lord Jesus. We are not merely members of a local church. We are part of a connectional body that includes members all over the world, as well as those who have finished their course and gone on before us. That is how vast and wide our communion of the saints is.

Communion begins with the Lord Jesus Christ. We are united with him. Communion also extends to all those who love the Lord. Our relationships with them have to grow out of our relationship with him, or else those relationships are hollow and empty.

The benefits are manifold. We get not only all the graces of Christ and fellowship with him, but also all the sharing of gifts and fellowship with other Christians. In addition, we have the right to pray for and with each other, the right to weep and rejoice together, and the right to unite in the work of building Christ's body, the church, as we believers make our vital contribution to the work of ministry.

The duties are obvious. We cannot be isolated from Christ, nor from other believers. They are as important to us as we are to them. They need us as we need them. We must not let anything disrupt our communion with Christ or one another whether it be grudges, misunderstandings, insensitivity, coldness, or anything else.

We are responsible for one another. Let us underscore this biblical truth as we proclaim the gospel. Salvation is not merely an individualistic proposition. It does not happen apart from the covenant family. We need the Lord but we also need each other. We need to cultivate a new sense of unity and community, if we are to be the church described in Scripture.

Chapter Twenty Seven
OF THE SACRAMENTS

CONFESSION OF FAITH

1. Sacraments are holy signs and seals of the covenant of grace, immediately instituted by God, to represent Christ, and his benefits; and to confirm our interest in him: as also, to put a visible difference between those that belong unto the church, and the rest of the world; and solemnly to engage them to the service of God in Christ, according to his Word.

2. There is, in every sacrament, a spiritual relation, or sacramental union, between the sign and the thing signified: whence it comes to pass, that the names and effects of the one are attributed to the other.

3. The grace which is exhibited in or by the sacraments rightly used, is not conferred by any power in them; neither doth the efficacy of a sacrament depend upon the piety or intention of him that doth administer it: but upon the work of the Spirit, and the word of institution, which contains, together with a precept authorizing the use thereof, a promise of benefit to worthy receivers.

4. There be only two sacraments ordained by Christ our Lord in the Gospel; that is to say, baptism, and the Supper of the Lord: neither of which may be dispensed by any, but by a minister of the Word lawfully ordained.

5. The sacraments of the old testament, in regard of the spiritual things thereby signified and exhibited, were, for substance, the same with those of the new.

THE CHRISTIAN FAITH is mystical in the sense that we walk by faith, not by sight. But how common a thing it is for us in our sinful condition to want signs. We want to see and then believe.

There was a time when signs in the miraculous sense accompanied the preaching of the prophets and apostles. They demonstrated the power, presence, and truth of God in what was being proclaimed. The historical Christian position maintains that these truth-conveying signs ceased with the death of the last apostle, simply because God has set forth his truth in the Holy Scriptures and given his Holy Spirit to enlighten and illumine our understanding of the Scriptures.

Does this mean there are now no signs to which we can point to give visible objectivity to our faith? Does this mean that signs are off limits to us? Of course not, if we follow God's order.

He has now established signs and seals as demonstrated means of setting forth the Christian faith. Those signs are referred to categorically as sacraments. In this restricted use of signs, the church in both Old and New Testament periods have had two.

Let's look at this section with that in mind. Starting with paragraphs four and five of chapter Twenty-Seven, we are reminded that there are two sacraments only—baptism and the Lord's Supper—which are to be carefully administered only by those lawfully ordained to dispense them.

Point one is important, especially with today's loose approach to so many things. There are only two sacraments, not three as some modernists proclaim, nor seven as Catholicism advocates. Baptism and the Supper of the Lord are the only two. They are to be administered by men called and ordained to that purpose. This is contrary to some fundamentalist and some Roman Catholic emphases, which allow unordained men or women to administer one or more sacraments.

This also has implications in some Reformed circles, where attempts are made to license laymen to preach the Word and administer sacraments. This position of paragraph four does have biblical warrant (Matt. 28:19; 1 Cor. 11:20, 23).

Point two: Paragraph five maintains that the things signified in the Old Testament counterparts to our sacraments, circumcision and the Passover meal, are the same as those in the New Testament. The difference, of course, is that Christ is now the one-for-all sacrifice. No more blood is to be shed. He finished that task. Hence, the New Testament forms have to be "non-blood" sacraments while reminding us of the blood atonement.

There is continuity in the Old and New Testament signs, as you would expect because the church in both periods is a continuation of the body for whom Christ died.

Point three: Paragraph one explains why God gave sacraments to his church and why they are important. They were instituted by God's command, not by man's invention. The sacraments represent Christ and his benefits visibly. They express our interest in him, and they distinguish believers from nonbelievers. They are brands of identification.

That is a good point to remember in case you are confronted with those who believe the sacraments may be privately or secretly observed. They lose their significance and meaning in private practice. They represent a visible difference between the church and world; hence, there is no need for us to set ourselves apart by such actions as disfiguring our faces or painting ourselves. The sacraments set us apart well enough. They are like an engagement ring on a woman's finger. She is engaged to be married. So it is with each believer, as the sacraments are signs of our engagement to be the Lord's.

Point four: Baptism has no saving power; nor does the Lord's Supper. Paragraph two says, "There is, in every sacrament, a spiritual relation, or sacramental union, between the sign and the thing signified . . . ."

The word "engage" is used in paragraph one, but not the word "guarantee." There are those who believe that the sacraments are essential for salvation. There are those who believe that receiving the sacraments is an indisputable mark of redemption. These people are called *sacerdotalists.* Receiving the sacraments is no guarantee that the recipient will be saved, because that would be salvation by works. Only Christ can save.

Baptism is a water application that signifies cleansing. It doesn't cleanse. It points to cleansing in the blood of Christ. It is spoken of as a "washing" in Titus 3:5. Our cleansing may or may not be tied to the moment of water application. We have no guarantee either way. The timing belongs to God.

The Lord's Supper containing bread and wine are merely symbols of Christ's body and blood. They do not *become* his body and blood. The supper is not bloody; it is a sign of his shed blood. "The names and effects of the one [the element] are attributed to the other [the body or blood]," according to paragraph two.

The recipient of either sacrament does not receive saving grace by the sacraments. There are people in hell today who received both sacraments.

Judas Iscariot is one example. Esau, who received circumcision, would appear to be another.

Point five: Roman Catholicism affirms that when the sacraments are properly administered, the individual receives grace. Not so, according to the Westminster Standards' understanding of Scripture.

Another important point, especially in light of paragraph four, is that the meaning of the sacraments and the blessings they bring are not dependent on the person who administers the sacraments. While some would make the minister the key, our standards rightly direct our attention to the Holy Spirit and his work. The sacraments are signs that need spiritual discernment; therefore, our attention must be focused on the Holy Spirit and the Word of institution (many say "words of institution").

"The word of institution" is an important phrase. The reading of Scripture to introduce the sacraments explains their meaning so that those in attendance will not have wrong ideas about the sacraments. Without Scripture and the Holy Spirit, the sacraments are empty and meaningless.

When the sacraments are used in light of Scripture, with dependence on the Holy Spirit, and when those who partake do so worthily, there is promised benefit. Why? Because of the relationship between the sign and the thing signified.

The Christian faith has its signs. Sacramentally, there are two, baptism and the Lord's Supper. We could say there are three visible signs—baptism and the Lord's Supper plus the Scriptures of the Old and New Testaments. Those three give tangible evidence of the reality of the Christian faith.

The following two chapters of the Westminster Confession concentrate on the individual sacraments. Each is important and should not be neglected. While they have no saving power to convey in themselves, God does intend for his children to be marked as his and to receive all his benefits. Let us therefore use the sacraments to that end.

Chapter Twenty Eight
OF BAPTISM

CONFESSION OF FAITH

1. Baptism is a sacrament of the new testament, ordained by Jesus Christ, not only for the solemn admission of the party baptized into the visible church; but also, to be unto him a sign and seal of the covenant of grace, of his ingrafting into Christ, of regeneration, of remission of sins, and of his giving up unto God, through Jesus Christ, to walk in newness of life. Which sacrament is, by Christ's own appointment, to be continued in his church until the end of the world.

2. The outward element to be used in this sacrament is water, wherewith the party is to be baptized, in the name of the Father, and of the Son, and of the Holy Ghost, by a minister of the gospel, lawfully called thereunto.

3. Dipping of the person into the water is not necessary; but baptism is rightly administered by pouring, or sprinkling water upon the person.

4. Not only those that do actually profess faith in and obedience unto Christ, but also the infants of one, or both, believing parents, are to be baptized.

5. Although it be a great sin to contemn or neglect this ordinance, yet grace and salvation are not so inseparably annexed unto it, as that no person can be regenerated, or saved, without it; or, that all that are baptized are undoubtedly regenerated.

6. The efficacy of baptism is not tied to that moment of time wherein it is administered; yet, notwithstanding, by the right use of this ordinance, the grace promised is not only offered, but really exhibited, and conferred, by the Holy Ghost, to such (whether of age or infants) as that grace belongeth unto, according to the counsel of God's own will, in his appointed time.

7. The sacrament of baptism is but once to be administered unto any person.

IN ITS CONSTITUTION, the Presbyterian Church in America states that "children of believers are, through the covenant and by right of birth, non-communing members of the church. Hence they are entitled to baptism . . ." (Book of Church Order 6-1). Why such a statement in the constitution?

This provision, in a chapter defining membership, reflects a doctrine spelled out in paragraph four of The Westminster Confession of Faith's Chapter Twenty-Eight. It states, "Not only those that do actually profess faith in and obedience unto Christ, but also the infants of one, or both, believing parents, are to be baptized." This is not incidental or optional; it is an integral part of the denomination's theology. Baptism of believers and their children is a tradition within the Presbyterian and Reformed family, but it is a tradition rooted firmly in the Bible.

Why is it for children as well as for professing adults? For some, it is no more than a service dedicating the infant. Hence, non-Reformed churches have "christening" or naming ceremonies. While the rite is conducted in a church ordinarily, little spiritual significance is attached.

At the other extreme are those who claim that baptism causes the new birth. One's spiritual birthday is the day of baptism, in their view. Interestingly, within the camp of those who believe this are some who baptize only mature persons making their own professions of faith ("believer's baptism") as well as those who baptize infants.

Two technical terms are used in sermons or books about this question: *baptismal regeneration* and *presumptive regeneration*. Baptismal regeneration ties the new birth to the moment of baptism. Presumptive regeneration presumes that a child is regenerate (born again) because his parents are Christians. Outstanding Christians through the years have strongly advocated one or the other of these positions.

Here again the beauty of the Westminster Confession's balance is obvious. Instead of going to either extreme, it keeps truth in perspective. It doesn't involve itself in scholastic argument for which Scripture has no answer. It leaves off idle speculation and deals only in formulating the Bible's position.

That position is, simply, that baptism is for adult believers and their children. Even if only one parent is a professing Christian, the children are to be baptized (following Paul's words in 1 Corinthians 7:14, for instance).

What exactly is baptism? Paragraph one's answer is excellent. It is a bit more detailed than the response to Shorter Catechism question 94, but it is briefer than the response to Larger Catechism question 165.

Baptism is a sacrament. What is that? Chapter Twenty-Seven defines sacraments as signs and seals of God's saving grace. Chapter Twenty-Eight's first paragraph elaborates. The purposes of baptism are to signify admission of the recipient to the visible church as well as to be a sign and seal of the covenant of grace, of his ingrafting into Christ, of his regeneration, of remission of sins, and of newness of life.

As paragraph three of Chapter Twenty-Seven states, the things signified in the sacraments depend on the work of the Holy Spirit to make them real. The things mentioned in the paragraph above are certainly signified in baptism, but the experience and understanding of them comes from the Holy Spirit "in his appointed time" (paragraph six).

The sacrament of baptism does not in itself cleanse, but signifies cleansing in Christ's blood. One's hope of salvation must not be based on baptism; the rite has no saving power. That power belongs to Christ alone, not to a ceremony.

Water, administered in the name of the Father, the Son, and the Holy Spirit, is the element to be used in baptism. The Triune God is the authority for baptism. Following both Old Testament and New Testament practices of specified people doing certain things, the sacrament is to be administered only by a minister of the gospel, lawfully (biblically) called to that office.

How is water to be administered? Dipping, pouring, and sprinkling are possible, but the confession mentions only pouring and sprinkling as correct modes.

Much has been said and could be said about mode of baptism, but this space could not handle all the arguments. We can say that the confession's position reflects both a safer interpretation of Scripture and good historical evidence that pouring and sprinkling were the New Testament practices. These practices of pouring and sprinkling were continued across the Reformation until the Anabaptists broke away from the Lutheran and Calvinistic families. Not only did Anabaptists deny the validity of the

Reformation's emphasis on infant baptism, but they insisted on dipping as *the* mode. (A study of Heb. 9:10ff would help those interested in pursuing the issue of mode of baptism.)

Paragraph five underscores the importance of the sacraments: "Although it be a great sin to condemn or neglect this ordinance, yet grace and salvation are not so inseparably annexed unto it, as that person can be regenerated, or saved, without it: or, that all that are baptized are undoubtedly regenerated." This paragraph makes four helpful points: 1) It is a sin to neglect this ordinance (simply because Christ said to do it); 2) It does not guarantee one's salvation (only Christ's shed blood does that); 3) It is not a necessary part of regeneration (the new birth cannot be linked to the application of water); and, 4) Not every recipient of baptism is finally saved (Acts 8:13, 23).

We claim for the sacrament only what Scripture claims. It is a sign and a seal. It visibly manifests the saving grace of God offered to his own. There is great blessing in the proper administration of it. The church is blessed. The believers are blessed. Their children are blessed. It is a visible proclamation of the gospel, which conveys the message of salvation to those who trust in Jesus alone for redemption.

Unlike the sacrament of the Lord's Supper, which is to be repeated often and regularly, baptism is to be administered only once. More than one baptism is not only unnecessary, but not in keeping with the Word of God.

Chapter Twenty Nine
OF THE LORD'S SUPPER

CONFESSION OF FAITH

1. Our Lord Jesus, in the night wherein he was betrayed, instituted the sacrament of his body and blood, called the Lord's Supper, to be observed in his church, unto the end of the world, for the perpetual remembrance of the sacrifice of himself in his death; the sealing all benefits thereof unto true believers, their spiritual nourishment and growth in him, their further engagement in and to all duties which they owe unto him; and, to be a bond and pledge of their communion with him, and with each other, as members of his mystical body.

2. In this sacrament, Christ is not offered up to his Father; nor any real sacrifice made at all, for remission of sins of the quick or dead; but only a commemoration of that one offering up of himself, by himself, upon the cross, once for all: and a spiritual oblation of all possible praise unto God, for the same: so that the popish sacrifice of the mass (as they call it) is most abominably injurious to Christ's one, only sacrifice, the alone propitiation for all the sins of his elect.

3. The Lord Jesus hath, in this ordinance, appointed his ministers to declare his word of institution to the people; to pray, and bless the elements of bread and wine, and thereby to set them apart from a common to an holy use; and to take and break the bread, to take the cup, and (they communicating also themselves) to give both to the communicants; but to none who are not then present in the congregation.

4. Private masses, or receiving this sacrament by a priest, or any other, alone; as likewise, the denial of the cup to the people, worshiping the elements, the lifting them up, or carrying them about, for adoration, and the reserving them for any pretended religious use; are all contrary to the nature of this sacrament, and to the institution of Christ.

5. The outward elements in this sacrament, duly set apart to the uses ordained

by Christ, have such relation to him crucified, as that, truly, yet sacramentally only, they are sometimes called by the name of the things they represent, to wit, the body and blood of Christ; albeit, in substance and nature, they still remain truly and only bread and wine, as they were before.

6.   That doctrine which maintains a change of the substance of bread and wine, into the substance of Christ's body and blood (commonly called transubstantiation) by consecration of a priest, or by any other way, is repugnant, not to Scripture alone, but even to common sense, and reason; overthroweth the nature of the sacrament, and hath been, and is, the cause of manifold superstitions; yea, of gross idolatries.

7.   Worthy receivers, outwardly partaking of the visible elements, in this sacrament, do then also, inwardly by faith, really and indeed, yet not carnally and corporally but spiritually, receive, and feed upon, Christ crucified, and all benefits of his death: the body and blood of Christ being then, not corporally or carnally, in, with, or under the bread and wine; yet, as really, but spiritually, present to the faith of believers in that ordinance, as the elements themselves are to their outward senses.

8.   Although ignorant and wicked men receive the outward elements in this sacrament; yet, they receive not the thing signified thereby; but, by their unworthy coming thereunto, are guilty of the body and blood of the Lord, to their own damnation. Wherefore, all ignorant and ungodly persons, as they are unfit to enjoy communion with him, so are they unworthy of the Lord's table; and cannot, without great sin against Christ, while they remain such, partake of these holy mysteries, or be admitted thereunto.

MUCH DEBATE has developed in church circles recently over the Lord's Supper. What is it? Who is it for? Who is it not for?

One denomination in the Presbyterian family officially allows participation in the Lord's Supper by some who are not yet communing members of the church. Some members have departed from their churches over this issue.

One expects controversy over such an important matter. This was why the writers of the Westminster Confession of Faith expressed their position on the Lord's Supper the way they did.

Chapter Twenty-Nine is important. It gives the background and meaning of this sacrament. It defines what it is and who it is for. It underscores what happens during the meal and the danger of participating wrongly.

In the church we always have had two sacraments. In the Old Testament form they were circumcision and the Passover. In the New Testament the forms were changed to baptism and the Lord's Supper. Why the change?

Basically, there is to be no more bloody sacrifice. Jesus' blood was shed once for all. The sacrament is to be a perpetual reminder of Jesus' sacrifice on the cross, and there is to be no bloodshed.

In this sacrament believers' benefits are sealed. They are nourished spiritually. They grow in grace as a result of proper observance. They experience and express a common bond with others who are members of Christ's mystical body.

No other activity of the Christian life carries with it the strong warning that this does. What happens to make the Lord's Supper so important? Unlike the teaching of the Roman Catholic Church regarding the Mass, Christ is not re-sacrificed. This supper is not a real sacrifice. But it is intended to commemorate Jesus' death on the cross. For Rome or anyone to suggest the need for further sacrifice is an affront to the concept of Christ's once-for-all sacrifice. To suggest a reinstitution of the sacrificial system is an abomination, and contrary to what Christ accomplished.

The Lord's Supper points to Christ's sufficient atonement for the sins of God's elect. Paragraph three speaks of the person who administers the supper and those who receive it. Ministers are to declare his Word and to serve the communion elements. Though some churches allow laymen to preach and administer the sacraments, the Presbyterian Church in America's position is that only those appointed to the office of minister of the Word have that privilege. The minister is to present the elements to those communicants present. Note two things, especially in light of current controversy.

First, only communicant members are to be served. It is for those who have made a credible public profession of faith in Jesus Christ, not their children, though they are in the covenant. Why? Because Paul warns in 1 Corinthians 11 that those who participate must believe and understand.

Second, there is no private communion: "... but to none who are not then present in the congregation." Those professing Christians who are present are the only ones to receive the sacraments, according to paragraph three.

What about the elements of the supper? Bread and wine. A certain kind of bread and wine? No. People err when they begin arguing this point. Should one use leavened or unleavened bread, wine or juice? The confession says "bread and wine." Could we paraphrase and say "bread and the fruit of the vine" and not get sidetracked on any other issue? Both bread and wine are essential to the supper because of the Lord's ordination.

The Roman Catholics advocate a doctrine called *transubstantiation*. The Lutherans hold to the doctrine of *consubstantiation*. Transubstantiation means that at the time of the Mass the bread and the wine are "magically" transformed into the body and blood of the Lord. Thus he is re-sacrificed. None dare spill on the floor. It is literally a bloody Mass.

Advocates of consubstantiation believe that while the bread and wine remain just that, at the words of consecration the real body and blood of Christ, though not visible, are really present in, with, and under the bread and wine.

The Westminster Confession states that neither of these positions is true. Though the bread and wine are symbolically referred to as the Lord's body and blood, they remain only bread and wine. Their relationship to Christ's body and blood is a symbolic one.

There is nothing superstitious or magical in the Lord's Supper. There is only a symbolic connection; yet, it is a most significant connection. For the worthy believer feeds on the crucified Christ and all his benefits, according to paragraph seven. Christ is spiritually present at the supper. Imagine the implications of feeding on him if either transubstantiation or consubstantiation was valid.

This is a spiritual sacrament, and only has meaning for those spiritually alive. Paragraph eight mentions that sometimes, maybe often, wicked and ignorant men receive the outward elements, but they do not receive the benefits. There is no magical spirituality that comes upon those who partake. There is on the one hand deep judgment for the unworthy—weakness, sickness, and death. On the other hand, there is real blessing to the worthy.

Unbelievers or even unrepentant believers are not worthy of the Lord's blessing; hence, they do not find it. It is even a great sin against Christ to partake of the holy mysteries of this sacrament unworthily.

This is a point that those churches that allow non-communing members to take this supper must consider. There is a warning to parents who allow their children to take the supper elements without faith and understanding. There is a warning to unrepentant individuals who take these elements. However, the confession underscores the blessing that comes to those who receive the sacrament worthily. Christ's spiritual presence becomes one of the particular blessings experienced during the supper.

Chapter Thirty
OF CHURCH CENSURES

CONFESSION OF FAITH

1. The Lord Jesus, as King and Head of his church, hath therein appointed a government, in the hand of church officers, distinct from the civil magistrate.

2. To these officers the keys of the kingdom of heaven are committed; by virtue whereof, they have power, respectively, to retain, and remit sins; to shut that kingdom against the impenitent, both by the Word, and censures; and to open it unto penitent sinners, by the ministry of the gospel; and by absolution from censures, as occasion shall require.

3. Church censures are necessary, for the reclaiming and gaining of offending brethren, for deterring of others from the like offenses, for purging out of that leaven which might infect the whole lump, for vindicating the honor of Christ, and the holy profession of the gospel, and for preventing the wrath of God, which might justly fall upon the church, if they should suffer his covenant, and the seals thereof, to be profaned by notorious and obstinate offenders.

4. For the better attaining of these ends, the officers of the church are to proceed by admonition; suspension from the sacrament of the Lord's Supper for a season; and by excommunication from the church; according to the nature of the crime, and demerit of the person.

THIS CHAPTER is extremely important to the life and discipline of the church. It is at this point that one could have wished for the preciseness demonstrated with other subjects. The confession makes a good general statement, but the Bible is much more precise on church government.

We believe that the representative form of government known as Presbyterianism is the structure God established for his church. A government by elders (later incorporating the office of deacon) seems to be particularly clear in Scripture, though not developed in this chapter.

We will deal only with the principles set forth, with possible implications. The first paragraph establishes that the Lord Jesus is the King and Head of the church. The church is his body. It belongs to Him.

Christ is bodily in heaven and spiritually present on earth, so the church has men to oversee and lead it. Christ has established in his Word the way in which his church is to be structured. He has appointed officers to govern his church who are distinct from the civil magistrate.

We learn two things from the first paragraph: **First**, the church of the Lord Jesus Christ has a government; **second**, that government is not the civil magistrate's. The church officers rule in the church; the civil officers rule in matters of state. Though advice may be exchanged by the two, church and state separation is Christ's intent for his church.

We recommend reading the book *Biblical Church Government*, by Don K. Clements, for a more detailed study in this area. The book explains government by appointed officers under Christ the Head of his church, and explains the biblical basis for the PCA two-office position.

Paragraph two elaborates on the authority and responsibility of the ruling officers. This is important because often we fail to appreciate the fullness of their responsibilities.

The confession picks up on Scripture in Matthew 16:19, where reference is made to the keys of the kingdom of heaven being given to the leaders—first to the apostles and now to the board of elders, or Session.

Keys are symbols of authority in the Bible, and their mention here indicates that the officers holding the keys in the church have the power or authority (1) to retain and remit sins, (2) to shut the kingdom against all unrepentant sinners by using both the Word and censures, (3) to open the kingdom to penitent sinners by the ministry of the gospel, and (4) to absolve from censures.

Here a distinction should be carefully noted because of frequently raised questions. What right do elders have to take such a stand where one's church membership is at stake? One response would be to say that they are elders, and thus have authority in themselves. However, the more satisfying answer would be that they have authority because they have the keys committed to them. The authority is in the keys and not in the elder himself.

The holder of the keys has responsibility to see that no unrepentant sinner be allowed the privileges and means of grace available only for the repentant sinner. He must make a judgment regarding a member's spiritual life. He must see to it that sacraments are not profaned and that unrepentant people abstain from them. He does this as an officer to whom God has given the keys of the kingdom.

He is responsible for the ministry of the gospel, which invites sinners to believe in Jesus Christ and repent of their sins, and for bringing in to the church such as are saved. He is also responsible for use of the Word and censures to exclude from the Lord's Table those who openly deny Christ or practice sin. With the Word of God he warns and with censures he acts.

As an officer in the Lord's church, he also has the authority to remove censures when repentance has been demonstrated.

Paragraph three explains why church discipline (both positive and negative) is essential. Five reasons are listed: (1) for reclaiming and gaining offending brethren; (2) for deterring others from similar sins; (3) for purging unbelief that would infect the whole body; (4) for vindicating the honor of Christ and the holy profession of the gospel; (5) for averting the wrath of God that might justly fall on the church if sin were left unchecked.

Whether or not a church enjoys the blessings and power of God is often determined by the church officers' execution of their responsibilities. God's blessings are not poured out on unbelief, rebelliousness, and indifference. The officers are the key deterrent to such in a local church.

Church discipline, even in its negative form, is no optional matter. It must be executed in a manner that reflects God's intended purpose as outlined in paragraph two.

Paragraph four explains how the elders should proceed with the administration of discipline. Jesus gave the overall formula in Matthew 18:15–17. The confession and our Book of Church Order, seeking to apply the Matthew 18 methods, point out that when censure is called for, steps should be taken in the following order: (1) admonition (warning); (2) suspension from the Lord's Supper for a season; and (3) excommunication, if neither admonition nor suspension reclaims the erring brother.

The Lord instructs us not to kick a brother when he is down, but rather to seek to lift him up. However, if he refuses and remains unrepentant, he is to be dealt with more severely. The ultimate step in discipline is excommunication, or as Jesus said, "Treat him as you would a pagan or a tax collector" (Matt. 18:17). (See also Book of Church Order Chapter 27, which details the process of discipline.)

We have seen the scars left in churches and denominations that have neglected the responsibilities spelled out in this section. We have also seen the fruits of revival and reformation in other churches and denominations where church members and officers have faithfully executed their duties.

Discipline is essential for healthy life and growth of the church. This chapter reflects the biblical concept of discipline. Church discipline is a positive effort to promote purity and holiness. The negative aspect comes when there is no positive response. One might be more consistent to view the entire area of discipline in a positive light.

Chapter Thirty also reminds us of two things. First, we must follow the Word of the King and Head of the church. We are to be obedient to him. Second, we must remember that the church officers' authority does not rest in them personally, but as the holders of God's keys by virtue of the office to which they were ordained.

In conclusion, one word of reminder needs to be sounded. It is the responsibility of each church member to seek to reclaim an erring brother. We are our brother's brother, but the elders have a particular responsibility in this area. They exercise their authority for the sake of the glory and purity of the body and the spiritual life of the members.

Chapter Thirty One
OF SYNODS AND COUNCILS

CONFESSION OF FAITH

1. For the better government, and further edification of the church, there ought to be such assemblies as are commonly called synods or councils: and it belongeth to the overseers and other rulers of the particular churches, by virtue of their office, and the power which Christ hath given them for edification and not for destruction, to appoint such assemblies; and to convene together in them, as often as they shall judge it expedient for the good of the church.

2. It belongeth to synods and councils, ministerially to determine controversies of faith, and cases of conscience; to set down rules and directions for the better ordering of the public worship of God, and government of his church; to receive complaints in cases of maladministration, and authoritatively to determine the same: which decrees and determinations, if consonant to the Word of God, are to be received with reverence and submission; not only for their agreement with the Word, but also for the power whereby they are made, as being an ordinance of God appointed thereunto in his Word.

3. All synods or councils, since the Apostles' times, whether general or particular, may err; and many have erred. Therefore they are not to be made the rule of faith, or practice; but to be used as a help in both.

4. Synods and councils are to handle, or conclude nothing, but that which is ecclesiastical: and are not to intermeddle with civil affairs which concern the commonwealth, unless by way of humble petition in cases extraordinary; or, by way of advice, for satisfaction of conscience, if they be thereunto required by the civil magistrate.

YOU MAY HAVE heard it said that our Presbyterian Church in America is a church Reformed in faith and Presbyterian in polity. Or you may have picked up the phrase that we are both a confessional and a connectional church. Those statements are good brief descriptions of our denomination. The Westminster Confession of Faith sets forth in a concise way our Reformed system of doctrine. It also underscores some basics about the church's polity or type of government.

Chapter Thirty-One speaks to the issue of church government. In reading the four paragraphs, one is made aware that the church is broader than the local congregation. Each local church is a part of a broader or larger organization. No congregation is an island to itself.

Though this concept is often betrayed in practice, the principle of connectionalism nonetheless is Scripture's teaching. One has only to read such passages as 1 Timothy 4:14 and Acts 15 to see the church in its broader organizational aspect.

The confession summarizes this by saying, "For the better government, and further edification of the Church, there ought to be such assemblies as are commonly called Synods or Councils . . . ." No isolated congregation can experience the breadth of the Christian faith.

In Acts 15 we have a record of many churches being confronted with the important issue of church membership and its requirements. So for the better government and further edification of the church, the Jerusalem Council (or assembly) was convened. It was comprised of representatives from the local churches. The decisions made by that assembly were authoritative and binding on the local churches (see verses 28 and 29).

The risen King and Head of the church delegated authority to that assembly. This council met during the apostolic age, but such a procedure has been active in the church since that time.

In the biblical system of government adopted by the Presbyterian Church there is a gradation of courts. The local church court is ruled by elected elders. The presbytery and assembly (higher courts of appeal) are ruled by representatives from the local levels. The biblical system of church government is representative.

This is why it is a contradiction of terms to use "Presbyterian" and "independent" in the same phrase. Chapter Thirty-One sheds light as to why this is true.

Neither Scripture nor the confession gives a detailed outline of the structure of such assemblies, nor does either mandate how often an assembly should meet. The confession merely states that there are synods, councils, or assemblies that should meet "as often as they shall judge it expedient for the good of the church."

It is obvious that such meetings are not merely for fellowship. Rather they are to deal with specific issues that either face the church or will face the church in the future.

Paragraph two lists a number of responsibilities of such assemblies: (1) to determine controversies of faith, (2) to determine cases of conscience, (3) to set down rules and directions for public worship, (4) to set down rules and directions for the government of the church, (5) to receive and act on complaints, and (6) to see that decisions are carried out.

The power of such assemblies depends on whether their decisions are agreeable with the Word of God. Local churches are to receive and act on decisions of the assemblies, insofar as they are agreeable to the Bible.

Notice the six things listed above. One is to receive and act on complaints. When a lower court cannot come to a decision or has reached a decision that has generated complaint from the people involved, the higher court can hear the case and render a verdict.

Other areas of authority involve the rules and directions for public worship and the government of God's church. Members of our denomination will understand why we have a Book of Church Order. That book has three sections: government, discipline, and worship. Paragraph two of Chapter Thirty-One of the confession gives an idea why those three areas are part of our church's constitution.

Notice also that such assemblies have the power to determine controversies of faith. While some have been of the opinion that church councils should only act on judicial cases in process, the confession grants assemblies the power to deal with such issues that would cause controversy in the church if left alone.

Our own assembly has utilized this right on several occasions by addressing issues for which there were no cases in process, such as: the charismatic movement, abortion, reconstructionism (theonomy), and marriage and divorce. The assembly in each instance sought to speak the mind of God as set forth in Scripture on either issues that were judged divisive, or inquiries from people seeking clarification from Scripture in order to avert controversy.

Paragraph three wisely states that assemblies may err in their conclusions. They do not speak with divine authority; therefore, assembly pronouncements are not to be the rule of faith (that belongs to Scripture alone), but they are to be used in understanding and interpreting the rule of faith. One should be reminded that the truth of God is not to be privately interpreted.

As we studied in Chapter One, paragraph ten, the confession teaches that the final authority in all matters of religion is the Holy Spirit speaking in the Scriptures. Only God and his Word are infallible.

The fourth paragraph is careful to point out the jurisdiction and power of such church assemblies. Just as the civil government cannot order the church's affairs, neither can the church dictate policy to the civil authorities. This paragraph is a warning that has gone unheeded by many who claim allegiance to the Westminster Standards.

Some of us have come from church backgrounds that adhere to this concept in principle but not always in practice. Courts of these churches have adopted positions that "intermeddle" with civil authorities regarding political, economic, and military matters, among others.

Our American edition of the confession emphasizes the validity of separation of church and state, but not with the intent for civil authorities to leave God and his Word out of their decision-making process. Therefore, the church may by "humble petition in cases extraordinary; or, by way of advice, for satisfaction of conscience, if [it] be thereunto required by the civil magistrate," speak its mind to the civil government.

These two institutions of authority, church and state, are to operate under God's sovereign will. Each has its own responsibility in carrying out the will of God. Neither is to usurp the other's authority. Both may give advice but neither has the God-given right to exceed its limits. Both civil and ecclesiastical leaders should acknowledge, appreciate, and practice this principle. The hope is that there will be mutual cooperation as each seeks to carry out the will of God.

Of course the church has a right to speak out when the government seeks to overstep its bounds, as was attempted in San Francisco some years ago when a church's right to dismiss a homosexual organist was challenged in the civil courts. Likewise, civil magistrates have grounds to complain against such religious organizations as the World Council and the National Council of Churches when they seek political power.

The church and religious leaders do have a responsibility and a right to speak out on definite moral issues, but this paragraph teaches how far we may go and what methods we have at our disposal in carrying out our God-given tasks.

Chapter Thirty Two

OF THE STATE OF MEN AFTER DEATH, AND OF THE RESURRECTION OF THE DEAD

CONFESSION OF FAITH

1. The bodies of men, after death, return to dust, and see corruption: but their souls, which neither die nor sleep, having an immortal subsistence, immediately return to God who gave them: the souls of the righteous, being then made perfect in holiness, are received into the highest heavens, where they behold the face of God, in light and glory, waiting for the full redemption of their bodies. And the souls of the wicked are cast into hell, where they remain in torments and utter darkness, reserved to the judgment of the great day. Besides these two places, for souls separated from their bodies, the Scripture acknowledgeth none.

2. At the last day, such as are found alive shall not die, but be changed: and all the dead shall be raised up, with the selfsame bodies, and none other (although with different qualities), which shall be united again to their souls forever.

3. The bodies of the unjust shall, by the power of Christ, be raised to dishonor: the bodies of the just, by his Spirit, unto honor; and be made conformable to his own glorious body.

CHAPTER THIRTY-TWO brings us to the most basic issue with which man has to come to grips. All men are concerned with the subject of death and the question, If a man die, will he live again?

Some would maintain that this life is all there is, and when a person's life on earth is over, he is done. Although those few would be comfortable if such a position were the reality, the truth is that each man has an inner knowledge that there is life beyond the grave.

Such knowledge may not always be conscious, but we know there is an afterlife or a life after this earthly life.

Much could be said to demonstrate this truth, but we shall devote our space to dealing with the areas covered in the Confession of Faith. What happens to the body and soul at death? What happens to those alive at the last day of history? What is different about the deaths of the righteous and the unrighteous?

The Bible teaches that death is a sign of God's judgment on sin. He created man to live; however, sin entered the picture and brought separation and death. Jesus Christ came to restore life by his death and resurrection. He succeeded with his work, and yet he allowed physical death to stand.

No believers except two, Enoch and Elijah, have gone to heaven without tasting death. "Man is destined to die once, and after that to face judgment . . ." (Heb. 9:27).

What happens at death to the body and soul? What happens during the time that Christ is preparing for his return? Let's deal with those aspects.

Here is an individual who comes to the end of his earthly life. What happens? His body is corrupted and returns to the dust. "Ashes to ashes, dust to dust."

The soul at the point of death doesn't sleep, nor cease to exist. It passes immediately into eternity. The souls of believers go to be with the Lord and are made perfect. Though some have taught that man's soul is not immortal, and though some have said that the soul merely falls asleep, Scripture teaches the truth. Paragraph one of Chapter Thirty-Two is a good summary.

While the bodies of the righteous and unrighteous die, the souls continue. However, while the souls of believers are in heaven, alive with the Lord and all the saints having arrived earlier, the souls of the wicked are cast into hell to suffer eternal torment. Those are the only alternatives—heaven or hell. There is no purgatory, no soul sleep, and no non-existence!

Jesus' words to the penitent criminal on the next cross regarding his being with Jesus in paradise that day is one of several passages that underscore this truth. There is no second chance after death. When death occurs, the person's destiny is confirmed. The Christian death is a departure to be with the Lord.

How should Christians react to death? We should have a twofold response. **First**, there should be joy over anyone going to be with the Lord.

Second, there should be apprehension about the grave because it is the final blow of pain. There should be joy and grief. But Paul said that the Christian's grief should be clothed in hope.

Christians also believe in the bodily return of Jesus Christ at the last day. But what will happen on that day to those who have not died? Paragraph two answers that question. You could read details in 1 Thessalonians and 1 Corinthians 15, but by way of summary the confession states, "such as are found alive shall not die, but be changed." Bodies in the grave shall be raised, the same bodies that were buried, only this time without corruption. Bodies and souls will be reunited, and we shall be with the Lord forever, body and soul. We believe in the resurrection of the body. We believe that we will have identity, substance, and form in eternity, and especially after the resurrection.

What about the bodies of the unjust? They too shall come forth from the grave by the power of Christ but only to be cast into hell, body and soul. The bodies of believers are raised to honor, those of the unbelievers to dishonor.

This is based on Christ's own death and bodily resurrection. That is the basis of our hope. Without it we are the most pitiable of all men, as Paul reminded the Thessalonians.

When we profess to believe in Jesus' bodily resurrection, we are also affirming hope in our own resurrection. Scripture gives those in Christ every reason to believe that there is far more to life than simply today. Even as we stand beside the grave of a fellow Christian, we remember that the believer's soul is with the Lord but the body must be sown in corruption. Yet, we also know that the body sown in corruption will be raised in incorruption. Eternal death has no power over believers.

What Christ offers his followers is glorious hope of everlasting life and immortality. We could technically say that only Christians have everlasting life and immortality.

What about unbelievers? Do the Scriptures and the confession teach that even they are immortal? Let's suggest that unbelievers have an eternal existence; however, it is not life. It is an eternal death. Christians live eternally body and soul. Non-Christians die eternally body and soul.

Christians die in hope. Non-Christians die without hope. Both shall die. Christ the Lord makes the difference. He alone can remove the sting and hurt of death, but only because he has gone before us to render death harmless to his followers.

The last section of the confession will amplify and explain the phrase, "the last day." We suggest that you read Chapters Thirty-Two and Thirty-Three together.

Chapter Thirty Three
OF THE LAST JUDGMENT

CONFESSION OF FAITH

1. God hath appointed a day, wherein he will judge the world, in righteousness, by Jesus Christ, to whom all power and judgment is given of the Father. In which day, not only the apostate angels shall be judged, but likewise all persons that have lived upon earth shall appear before the tribunal of Christ, to give an account of their thoughts, words, and deeds; and to receive according to what they have done in the body, whether good or evil.

2. The end of God's appointing this day is for the manifestation of the glory of his mercy, in the eternal salvation of the elect; and of his justice, in the damnation of the reprobate, who are wicked and disobedient. For then shall the righteous go into everlasting life, and receive that fullness of joy and refreshing, which shall come from the presence of the Lord; but the wicked who know not God, and obey not the gospel of Jesus Christ, shall be cast into eternal torments, and be punished with everlasting destruction from the presence of the Lord, and from the glory of his power.

3. As Christ would have us to be certainly persuaded that there shall be a day of judgment, both to deter all men from sin; and for the greater consolation of the godly in their adversity: so will he have that day unknown to men, that they may shake off all carnal security, and be always watchful, because they know not at what hour the Lord.

THE LAST CHAPTER of the Westminster Confession of Faith deals with a subject that is not very popular, either inside or outside the church. Judgment day has many ramifications that cause a diversity of reactions.

Some would be more comfortable to leave out this portion of the confession, and yet biblical doctrines are so interrelated that they stand or fall together. Each has an important relation to the whole. So it is with the doctrine of the last judgment.

We are aware of the diverse opinions and books written on this subject. Some have become fascinated by the study of last things. However, our approach must be neither neglect nor obsession. Balance is the key in any study of the Word. Relating each part to the whole is vital to a fuller understanding of God's revealed will or plan.

There is an aspect of history that is circular in pattern. Yet history does more than simply move in circles. If that is all there is to history, then maybe Albert Camus and other writers are on target in seeing the absurdity of life.

However, as we turn to Scripture we find that life is not absurd. History does not merely move in a circular pattern. It is moving closer and closer to a target day in which history, as we know it, will be over. Things will not always continue as they are. We are moving toward the day of judgment. Because that day is climactic, it is fitting that the Westminster Standards climax with that subject.

Notice as you read the three paragraphs of Chapter Thirty-Three how precisely the writers formulated this summary. Observe that subjects such as the millennium, which Christians have argued over for a long time, are omitted. What you have is a clear summation regarding Scripture's teaching on the judgment.

There are volumes and volumes written on other areas of eschatology (the study of end times), but our intention is to see what our standards say.

First, God has appointed a day of judgment. On that day, he will judge the world in righteousness. Judgment has been committed to Jesus Christ, the Lord and Savior. Notice the standard of judgment: it is neither man nor his works; rather, it is the righteousness of Jesus Christ.

On that day every person and angel will appear before God. Paragraph one emphasizes that the people who will stand before his throne of judgment are the apostate (fallen) angels and every person who has ever lived. At that time each will give an account or explanation to God for everything that he has ever said, thought, or done. Idle words, unconfessed sins, and any other transgressions of God's holy law will be brought into the open.

All persons and angels will receive from God what they deserve based on what they have done in the body, whether good or evil. No one will be acquitted on the basis of his intents or deeds. Only those in union with Jesus Christ will be justified.

On that day all of those seeing God will reveal or bring to light every deed, thought, and word. Moreover, no alibis or rationalizations will suffice. Only those with complete faith and trust in Jesus Christ will be saved.

Matthew 25:31–46 and Revelation 20:11–15 are among many passages that elaborate on the judgment day. You also could read 1 Corinthians 15 and 1 Thessalonians 4.

Several passages of Scripture, such as the one about wise and foolish virgins in Matthew Chapter 25, are given to remind us that judgment day is coming and that our responsibility is not to seek to outguess God but rather to be watchful and expect the Lord's return. One can readily see how the warning and promise of God's return will indeed be a deterrent to sin. Maybe that could be cited as one reason for so much laxness and wickedness in our day. Maybe people have not been confronted with the truth about judgment day. Maybe, as in the days of Noah, they have convinced themselves that things will always continue as they are.

In summary, the confession echoes Scripture regarding the certainty of the coming day of judgment. That day will come quickly and unexpectedly to those not watching. When it does occur, it will involve every man and angel; none will escape. On that day everything will be brought to light. Those united to Jesus Christ by faith will be saved. Those outside that union will be lost. Those who have added works to their faith will be rewarded. Those who have neither the root nor the fruit of faith will be punished (Matt. 25:31–46).

"Inasmuch as he hath appointed a day in which he will judge the world in righteousness by the man whom he hath ordained; whereof he hath given assurance unto all men, in that he hath raised him from the dead" (Acts 17:31 ASV).

Paragraph two elaborates on the events and purpose of judgment day. The first and foremost is God's showing his mercy in the salvation of the elect. We have all sinned and yet God has made a way of escape. Jesus Christ is our only hope on judgment day. Those who move toward the throne merely trusting in their works will not be saved.

Jesus Christ will also show that he is God of justice. For those who choose to face judgment on any basis other than faith in Jesus Christ, he will judge on the basis of their thoughts, words, and deeds. None will meet his standards of righteousness; hence, such will be cast into hell. They are the reprobates—wicked and disobedient.

Those who will be saved by the mercy and grace of God will go on to everlasting life (heaven) to be with the Lord forever. They will at that time receive the fruition of the promise, "whoever lives and believes in me will never die" (John 11:26). The elect will enter the new heaven and new earth portrayed in Revelation 21 and 22. They will have full joy and refreshment.

The wicked, on the other hand, shall be cast into eternal torment and be punished with everlasting destruction and banishment from the presence of the Lord and his glory and power. Because of God's common grace even the wickedest of sinners has received some godly benefits in this life, but it will not be so on the day of judgment and afterward. Then it will be only torment, punishment, and eternal death.

The Larger Catechism's questions 89 and 90 would be worth reading in this connection. They bring in some other aspects of the judgment that amplify paragraph two of Chapter Thirty-Three.

Paragraph three shows that Christ Jesus wants us to be absolutely certain that judgment day is coming. It is inescapable for all men and angels. Why is it important for us to be certain that such a day will come?

1) To deter all men from sin. Each man will have to stand before God and receive his judgment. Sin will not go unpunished. "I will repay,' says the Lord" (Rom. 12:19).

2) To bring consolation to believers in adversity. A believer may have suffered unjustly in this life, but judgment day is the watershed. Those who are first will be last. Those who have gone unpunished in this life will not escape any longer. God's righteousness will be vindicated. This is where God's claim that vengeance belongs to him will come to fulfillment.

3) To remind us to turn away from all hopes of salvation apart from faith in Jesus Christ. As one is reminded of the day of judgment, he must also be reminded that his only hope of salvation is Jesus Christ and his righteousness. Beware of false security.

4) To be reminded that only God knows when judgment day will come. Men can speculate, set dates, and do similar things to pinpoint that day, but it is only known to God. As Jesus said, neither the Son nor the angels knew when that day would come (Mark 13:32).